Po of a Lawman

U.S. Deputy Marshal Heck Thomas

by

Bonnie Stahlman Speer

Reliance Press
Cover art by Frederick Olds

Also by Bonnie Speer:
Errat's Garden
Moments in Oklahoma History,
 A Book of Trivia
Hillback To Boggy
Sons of Thunder
Cleveland County (OK),
 Pride of the Promised Land
The Great Abraham Lincoln Hijack
The Killing of Ned Christie
Following the Call: Casey Grimes,
 Dustbowl Evangelist
Write Your Life Story
Miss Little Britches

All rights reserved.
Copyright, 1996, by Bonnie Stahlman Speer
Typesetting, cover, and design, Cheryl Hanlon

Library of Congress CIP Data
Speer, Bonnie Stahlman
Portrait of a Lawman, U.S. Deputy Marshal Heck Thomas
Includes Illustrations
 1. Civil War
 2. Indian Territory
 3. Oklahoma Territory
 4. Outlaw History
 5. Heck Thomas, Biography

LC 95-72480
ISBN: 0-9619639-3-X paper trade

Published by Reliance Press,
1400 Melrose Drive, Norman, OK 73069

*Dedicated to the memory of
Beth Thomas Meeks and the Three Guardsmen.*

CONTENTS

Foreword .... Page ix
1. An Unforgettable Character 1
2. Boy Courier in the Confederate Army 7
3. Life in Atlanta During Reconstruction 14
4. Express Messenger on the Texas Frontier 21
5. U.S. Deputy Marshal in Indian Territory 35
6. A Storybook Romance 47
7. Pursuing Ned Christie 53
8. Chasing Outlaws in Oklahoma Territory 59
9. The Bill Doolin Gang 70
10. City Marshal of Lawton 79
11. Fire Chief Thomas 93
12. Colonel Hawkins' Ordeal 102
13. Calm Before the Storm 106
14. The Declining Years 120
15. Into the Sunset 132
16. Aftermath 143
    Endnotes 147
    Bibliography 159
    Index 164

ILLUSTRATIONS

U.S. Deputy Marshal Heck Thomas	Frontispiece
Heck Thomas, 1871	20
Federal Court in Fort Smith	37
Judge Isaac Parker	87
Tulsa in 1891	50
Matie Mowbray	50
Ned Christie	54
Opening of Unassigned Lands	60
The Three Guardsmen	62
Bill Doolin	75
Oklahoma Land Openings	80
Lawton Townsite At Opening	86
Lawton's First Police Force	89
Heck Thomas, Fire Chief and Chief of Police	94
Wolf Hunt	108
Heck Thomas and Game Chickens	112
Harley and Beth Thomas	115
Lawton City Hall	122
Heck Thomas and Sons	136

FOREWORD

During the course of my thirty-something journalistic career, sometimes I read of authors who came upon a trunkful of documented material which someone wanted them to compile into a book. How wonderful, I always thought, finding all that material in one spot. How easy it would be to write a book under those circumstances. Then one day that very thing happened to me.

I had known Beth Thomas Meeks for about six years and during that time we became good friends. Having been a student of the Old West long before I met Beth, I knew well the colorful stories about her lawman father, "Heck" Thomas.

His biography had been written by a well-known author, but Mrs. Meeks felt that it left out the human side of her father's nature. She looked upon him as more than a cold-blooded man hunter as this book seemed to portray. She spoke of her father so often that one day I proposed to her that if she wasn't satisfied with his previous biography, why didn't we try writing another book? This way he could be remembered the way she wanted, as a warm and caring human being as well as a fearless lawman.

It was then that she pulled from under her bed the wonderful "trunk" of my dreams, although in this instance, the trunk came in the form of a plain-looking, somewhat battered, old suitcase that held the past within its cardboard walls.

I opened the suitcase carefully and found myself filled with euphoria as I reverently sorted through stacks of letters, day books, documents, and pictures, all of which had been touched and read by Heck Thomas himself in days gone by. Then my gaze fell upon the scrapbook compiled by Matie Mowbray

Thomas, Heck's wife. In the many clippings therein, she had immortalized her husband, a renowned lawman of territorial days, and the scrapbook was mine for the using. I could scarcely believe my good fortune.

But once I got into the material and started piecing Heck's story together, I came down to reality in a hurry, for I found myself facing an historian's nightmare. Few of the clippings were dated or listed a source of identification. It took months of struggling for me to sort all the bits of information into chronological order and to research a volume of other historical data and to extract Mrs. Meeks' memories from her. Some clippings in the suitcase I could never pinpoint their source exactly nor date them. Occasionally Mrs. Meeks found my research in conflict with her memories and voiced her negative opinion.

But at last, the book was finished, and I think we were both satisfied. I, in that it was as nearly exact as I, as a research historian, could make it, Mrs. Meeks in that it portrayed her father from the personal angle, revealing him as a warm personality as well as a capable lawman.

I always thought that Matie Mowbray Thomas, Heck's wife, should have written this book about him, but outside of publishing several articles following his death, that was all she ever wrote.

Heck Thomas was one of the greatest of lawmen, according to a recent Smithsonian traveling exhibit on U.S. deputy marshals. He did much to help make the western frontier a safe place to live. He should hold a lasting place in our hearts and in the history of the Old West.

My thanks especially to Beth Thomas Meeks. Without her help and the abundance of material she provided from her personal files, this book could not have been possible.

U.S. Deputy Marshal Heck Thomas. Courtesy Thomas Collection.

Chapter 1

An Unforgettable Character

A thin streak of light still hung in the western sky of Virginia on this first day of September 1862. The ragged Confederate soldiers sank back wearily along the flank they had been defending all day in the Battle of Chantilly. In back of the line, a twelve-year-old boy attached to the Georgia 35th Infantry could scarcely distinguish the color of their uniforms in the growing dusk. Smoke from the violent battle which had raged here for hours drifted in the air, filling his nostrils with its acrid sting.

From out of the growing darkness, a one-armed soldier on a magnificent black horse dashed up before the line of weary soldiers. He rode with the grace and ease of one well-trained. He held the reins draped over his shoulder and his sword in hand. He drew the black up sharply before the line.[1]

"What troops are these?" he called out in a strong, direct tone that none but a commander would use. The rider's empty sleeve swayed in the evening breeze, and his horse pranced restlessly at the restraint.

"Forty-ninth Georgia," replied a ragged soldier, saluting.

For a second, the one-armed soldier remained motionless, the pale light gleaming off his sword and the gold braid upon his coat. He wheeled his horse and jabbed spurs into its sides.

It was then that the long line of Georgia soldiers realized the situation. This was a blue-coated Yankee officer. Up and down the line, guns began cracking. Before the horse had gone two hundred yards, the rider fell. The horse circled and ran back into the Confederate lines where he was quickly captured.

The fallen rider, the soldiers soon learned, was Gen. Phillip Kearney, an old classmate of Gen. Robert E. Lee and a veteran of the Mexican War. Kearney's horse, its saddle and bridle, and Kearney's sword were taken to the back of the line and placed in charge of the twelve-year-old boy.

Later, at Harper's Ferry, General Lee called for the horse and Kearney's possessions to be sent through the line under a flag of truce to Kearney's widow. The boy brought the horse forward. As he stood under the observation of Gen. Robert E. Lee, his heart swelled. He felt this was the proudest moment of his life.

That boy was Henry A. "Heck" Thomas. He served as a courier to his uncle, Gen. Edward Lloyd Thomas, in the Confederate Georgia 35th Infantry during the Civil War. His experience there was to set the tone for the remainder of his life.

In the years that followed the war, Heck became a police officer in Atlanta, went to Texas where he worked as an express guard for the Texas Express Company, then his restless nature led him north to Indian Territory. Here, from 1886 to 1891, he was commissioned as a U.S. deputy marshal in "Hanging Judge" Isaac C. Parker's Federal Court of the Western District of Arkansas, Fort Smith. From 1891 to 1901, Heck held a commission under every U.S. marshal appointed in Oklahoma Territory. He served eight years as the first city marshal at Lawton, Oklahoma. After Oklahoma statehood, in his declining years, he again held a U.S. deputy marshal's commission in the Western District of Oklahoma.

Fearless, Heck was wounded six times during the course of his thirty-year law career. Reportedly, he killed eleven men during this time, according to his youngest daughter, Beth Thomas Meeks. But this was something he talked little about. In later years, the only time she recalled hearing him mention it, he said he had never killed anyone he didn't have to.

Heck Thomas' man hunting exploits have been much written about in the annals of the early West. Among the more notable tales were his taking of the Pink Lee gang, his fight with Sam Bass during a Texas Express robbery, his pursuit of the Dalton gang, and his killing of outlaw Bill Doolin.

During his time with Judge Parker's court, Heck was noted for arresting more prisoners at a time than any other deputy. In one trip when making his circuit through Indian Territory, he astounded court officials by bringing in forty-one prisoners handcuffed to his wagon. Nine of these men were later executed.[2]

During Oklahoma Territory days, Heck, together with fellow United States Deputy Marshals Bill Tilghman and Chris Madsen, racked up such a record of law enforcement that the three lawmen became known as "The Three Guardsmen."

Heck was also renowned as a crack shot. No outlaw could outdraw him, according to Beth. His guns always came up blazing when necessary, and he was known to be deadly accurate. The Fort Smith *Elevator* warned outlaws they better seek cover when the intrepid lawman headed their way.[3]

Some people claimed that Bill Tilghman and Chris Madsen—whom Beth and her sister, Harley, always referred to as "Uncle Bill" and "Uncle Chris"—were faster on the draw than Heck. They weren't, Beth spoke with assurance. Her father was the fastest. But all three men, she added, agreed that Reno Madsen, Chris Madsen's son, was just as quick as Heck.

Heck was, indeed, a man of exceptional skills and rare courage, one who dedicated his entire life to fighting the criminal element. Yet, while he was an extremely dangerous man where outlaws were concerned, to his family, he was the most gentle man they had ever known. Educated and cultured, at one time Heck planned on entering the Methodist ministry.

He was an extremely handsome man. He stood about six-feet tall. His dark eyes were exceptionally keen and he could size up a person—man or girl—immediately. He stood arrow-straight and had delicate hands and walked lightly on small feet. He spoke in a soft, Southern drawl. During Heck's younger days, his hair was black and he wore a curved handlebar-mustache. In later years, his hair turned silver and he wore his mustache short and kept it well-trimmed.

Heck always looked neat. Beth could not recall ever seeing him with stubble on his face. He dressed impeccably. Even when he didn't have but two suits to his name, he kept them clean and pressed.

When chasing outlaws, Heck habitually wore knee-length boots, corduroy trousers, a flannel shirt, and a broad-brimmed, white Stetson hat which he doffed to the ladies upon meeting them. Sometimes he wore a black Prince Albert coat, long with a slit up the back. Because of this, the other deputies teased him, calling him "Scissortail." But the coat served a useful purpose. Beneath it, Heck wore his Colt .45 tucked out of sight. In times of danger, he unbuttoned the coat should the need for quick action arise.

Heck neither smoked nor drank. The only time Beth could recall hearing him swear was once in their front yard when he dropped a rock on his toe. "Jesus H. Christ," he said, hopping around on one foot. Beth was really shocked, for she had never heard him use such language.

Heck was fun-loving, forever pulling jokes on others. Once, when Beth's half-brother Albert was sixteen, he broke his leg near the Fox and Sac Agency in Indian Territory. His father loaded him into a wagon to take him back to their home in Guthrie. In Stillwater, Heck stopped and bought a bottle of mule liniment and a sack of candy. While he rubbed the liniment on Albert's ankle to ease the pain, he told him if he didn't cry he could have the candy. But what got Albert the most was that Heck told a Stillwater newspaper reporter that Albert was a young outlaw whom he had shot and was taking to jail.[4]

Following the opening of the Comanche reservation in Oklahoma Territory to settlement, Heck moved his family to Lawton where he continued in law enforcement. Sometimes he'd take Beth out of school to go with him when he served papers in the surrounding towns.

One day they went on the train to a nearby town. While there, Heck left Beth with a friend while he tended to his business. On his return, Heck put her back on the train. He said, "There's a man out here that I want to talk to. I'll be in, in a minute. You go on and sit down."

He had the tickets, of course. Beth went in and sat down. Her father "didn't come and didn't come." Soon, the train started up, and Beth was scared. The conductor came to get her ticket. She was afraid he'd put her off the train. Almost frantic she said, "My father is out there by the depot and he has the tickets." At that moment, Heck stepped around the corner of the coach where he had been hiding, playing a trick on her.

But sometimes the joke fell back on Heck. His wife was an excellent cook, and Heck loved to eat. One morning, Matie was frying hot cakes for breakfast. She had a pan of sugar syrup boiling on the wood cook stove. Heck was getting ready to shave. He came into the kitchen and saw the pan of boiling liquid. He thought the pan contained water and knew Matie had it there for a purpose. But he slipped the pan off the stove and poured the contents into his washbowl.

Matie glimpsed what he was doing out of the corner of her eye and knew what would happen. But he had pulled enough pranks on her that she left him alone. Heck lathered up his face with the sugar syrup, and as Matie expected it gummed up his mustache. He had a terrible time getting the sticky stuff washed out. Matie, Harley, and Beth laughed and laughed.

Heck Thomas was a man of contrasting character. He could be a deadly man hunter feared by all, but at the same time, his family knew him to be a loving husband and father, gracious and full of fun. He was always a gentleman, courteous to all whom he met. As an officer of the law, he lived and acted as was expected of him. Judge Isaac Parker, according to Beth, always spoke of him in the highest terms in regard to his prowess as a lawman and his integrity as a man.

Heck Thomas never wrote much about his own experiences. Nor did he talk about outlaws and such to his daughters. He considered this something little girls didn't need to know. Matie always looked upon her husband with pride. She had an excellent memory and lovingly kept the scrapbook on his life. She wrote several articles about him after his death.

Chapter 2

Boy Courier in the Confederate Army

Henry Andrew "Heck" Thomas was born on January 6, 1850, Athens, Georgia. He was the twelfth and youngest child of Lovick Pierce Thomas and Martha Ann Fullwood Bedell, a former widow with three sons by her first marriage. Edward, Robert, and Pendleton Bedell each fought as young men in the Mexican War.

Heck inherited an illustrious ancestry on both sides of his family. When young, he sat around enthralled, listening to his family talk about their past, which greatly influenced his life. According to family records, his mother was a direct descendant of Pocohantas and James Rolfe of Virginia, who was among the first colonists in America.[1]

The Thomas family could trace its roots back to Mary Queen of Scots, the Duke of Norfolk, and Sir Thomas Holliday, Lord Mayor of London in 1605.[2]

Heck's great-great-great grandfather, Thomas Thomas, arrived in America in 1632 at the age of twenty-two. He became a judge in Patauxant, Maryland. Another relative, the Honorable Francis Thomas, became governor of that state and later served as a congressman. Other Thomas family members held office in their local legislatures. Judge Thomas' two sons, Phillip and Nathaniel, fought in the Revolutionary War.

After the war, Phillip Thomas, Heck's great-great-grandfather moved from Maryland to Virginia and later to Georgia. He settled first in Columbus in 1797, then relocated in Franklin County along with his youngest son, Edward Lloyd Thomas. Edward, Heck's great-grandfather, became a Methodist preacher and surveyor. He set the lines for what is much of Georgia today, including the town of Oxford, Georgia, where he settled.[3]

Reverend Thomas was described as a fine, gentle man, "who was not easily moved to criticize others . . . ."[4] Undoubtedly, he passed these traits on to his four surviving sons, Henry Phillip, Wesley Wailes, Lovick Pierce, and Edward Lloyd, Jr. All were well-educated, strong, firm young men who knew how to take command of a situation. Each of them grew up to become cultured, prominent Georgians, leaders in the communities where they lived.

Lovick Pierce Thomas, Heck's grandfather, was born March 12, 1812, in Franklin County, Georgia. His father named him for a friend who was a Methodist bishop. When a young man, Lovick established a plantation near Athens. He owned a number of slaves. Though not rich, his family was comfortably well off.

Lovick's older brother, Henry Phillip Thomas owned a large plantation near Lawrenceville.

The youngest son in the Thomas family, Edward Lloyd Jr., was born in Clarke County, Georgia, March 23, 1825. He graduated from Emory College in 1846. Years later, young Heck must have listened wide-eyed to how his Uncle Edward, in 1847 enlisted as a private in one of the Georgia calvary regiments that fought in the Mexican War at Vera Cruz and Mexico City. Pvt. Thomas was soon promoted to lieutenant for "conspicuous gallantry." In a daring charge, he captured Iturbide, a prominent officer on Santa Ana's staff. In 1848, the Georgia Legislature adopted a resolution commending Lt. Thomas for his gallantry.[5] The Secretary of War, George W. Crawford, offered him a lieutenancy in the regular army of the United States. But the young officer declined the offer. He returned home to marry Jennie Gray, a beautiful, young member of a leading and wealthy family in Talbot County, and to establish a large plantation near his brother Henry's at Lawrenceville, refusing many solicitations to enter politics.

In 1851, the year after Heck was born, his father and brother, Lovick Pierce, Jr., and Pen Bedell, who had been wounded in the Mexican War, made a trip to the California gold fields. They returned home none the richer, but with many adventurous tales to tell.

Reared in this atmosphere of uniforms, bold men, and courageous spirits, it was no wonder that young Heck yearned to follow in the footsteps of his father and uncles. In addition to his general education, Heck's mother saw to it that her youngest son received the ethics of good breeding and culture, things which Heck was to never forget. He attended the Methodist Church and Sunday School regularly. The district superintendent was a close friend of the Thomas family. With his influence and that of his grandfather, Reverend Thomas, Heck determined at an early age he would become a preacher.

In 1861, when Heck was eleven-years-old, the "War of Northern Aggression," as those in the South called it, broke out.[6] The Thomas men immediately heeded the call to arms in a manner worthy of their noted ancestors.

Heck's uncle, Edward Lloyd Thomas, Jr., was authorized by President Jeff Davis of the Confederacy to raise a regiment in Georgia. On October 15, 1861, Uncle Ed, as Heck always referred to him, was appointed colonel of the 35th Georgia Infantry.[7]

Armed only with flintlock guns, Thomas marched his command immediately into service at the Battle of Seven Pines, wherein he was wounded slightly. He was soon promoted to brigadier general. He served in this rank to the end of the war, fighting in almost every major battle. A close friend of General Lee, the Thomas family believed Uncle Ed might have succeeded to the command of Pender's Division after Gettysburg had not General Lee feared unrest between the brigades from North and South Carolina under the leadership of a Georgian.[8]

Another of Heck's uncles, Henry Phillip Thomas, raised a company of one hundred men at Lawrenceville. Soon, he was promoted to colonel in the Georgia 16th for gallantry in action. His four sons, Scott, Edward, Charley, and Henry became captains in the Confederate army. A second uncle, Wesley Wailes Thomas, attained the rank of major.

Heck's father, Lovick Pierce Thomas, and Pen Bedell joined Cobb's Legion and were sent to the Virginia Army. Officers soon sent Pen home because of his bad eyesight, which was caused by his wounds in the Mexican War. Undaunted, Pen raised another company of men and was assigned with them to Coast Service.

Lovick transferred to General Thomas' 35th Georgia Volunteers where he became well known as the "Fighting Quartermaster." Promoted to captain in the Virginia regiment, he continued in this capacity to the end of the war.

At the beginning of the war, Heck's brother Lovick, Jr., a twenty-six-year-old storekeeper at Lawrenceville, whom Heck always called "Bud," sold his stock of goods and organized Company A of the 42nd Regiment and marched off to fight.[9] In March 1892, when nearly all of the officers were killed on the bloody battlefield at Resaca, Bud was placed in command as colonel of the 42nd Georgian Infantry, Stovall Brigade.[10] He led this regiment until its last fight at Bentonville, and surrendered with it there. He fought in twenty-two battles, including Vicksburg where the men were in the trenches forty-seven days and nights, half-starved and poorly armed. Other Thomas men enlisted in the army by the score as privates.[11]

With all this patriotic fervor bustling about him, it was no wonder twelve-year-old Heck was wild to join the fighting, too. His application to enlist was turned down again and again because of his age. When his opportunity finally came, he was quick to grab it.[12]

During the fighting at Mechanicsville, Heck's father, Lovick Thomas, had been badly wounded, shot with a minnie ball through the right lung. He was sent back to Georgia to recuperate. In August 1862, when partially recovered, he returned to his command, taking with him two black servants, Riley and Johnson, to wait on him and Uncle Ed. Heck went along to serve as courier to his uncle.

At first, as Heck put it, he thought he was "there on a picnic." He confessed to being "in everybody's way."[13] But his picnic soon ended. He wrote to his brother Bud:[14]

> The second day after we got to pa's command the second battle of Manassas was fought. I thought I was pretty well in the midst of it. Well do I remember when I wrote home the pride I took in writing my address: 'Henry A. Thomas, thirty-fifth regiment Georgia volunteers, Thomas' brigade, A.P. Hill's division, Stonewall Jackson's corps.'
>
> Then if I could get hold of a soldier's envelope

11

carrying something like this printed on it I was happy—happier than wise:

> *Stand firmly by your cannon,*
> *Let ball and grapeshot fly,*
> *Trust in God and Davis*
> *And keep your powder dry.*

At the Second Battle of Manassas, twenty-five thousand men were killed. Heck witnessed this from behind the lines:

> We had been posted in a railroad cut which a command known as the Pennsylvania Buck Tails were trying to take. The federals charged up to the edge of the cut five times, but always they were rebuffed. For 500 yards, you could walk on dead men, some places two and three deep. Nearly all were shot in the face, neck or head. But the 35th held that cut just the same. They were Georgians to a man in that regiment.

A few days after the Second Battle of Manassas, the Battle of Chantilly, sometimes called "Ox Hill," was fought. It was here that Gen. Phillip Kearney was killed. Just after dark that night, a soldier came to the rear of the Confederate line leading Kearney's black horse with its saddle and bridle to where Heck was with the servants and his Uncle Ed's baggage. He gave the horse over to Heck's care.

The following day, General Lee requested permission to send the body of Kearney back to his family. But before this could be done, the troops of Gen. "Stonewall" Jackson crossed over into Maryland. They captured Harper's Ferry and Frederick City, taking fourteen thousand prisoners. While the battle raged at Sharpsburg, the task of holding these prisoners fell upon General Thomas' brigade. Heck wrote later, "We could see the smoke and hear the cannon from Harper's Ferry."[15]

While the troops were still at Harper's Ferry, General Lee sent for Kearney's horse. Heck proudly brought it forward. He had ridden the general's horse and had cared for it up to that time and he hated to part with it.

Heck stayed with his father and Uncle Ed for fourteen months, witnessing some of the bloodiest fighting in the Civil War. By then he had grown a lot in stature and wisdom. In later years, he said that by the time he was a little over thirteen-years-old, he could safely say he had seen ten thousand dead men. In particular he recalled one night after a big battle, when he went around the hospital tent where doctors had been amputating limbs. In the dark he stepped in arms and legs up to his knees.

Heck's military career came to an abrupt halt in the winter of 1863. He contracted typhoid fever, and was sent home, in his words, "dead to the world."[16]

Chapter 3

Life in Atlanta During Reconstruction

Sometime during the early part of the Civil War, Lovick Thomas moved his family to Atlanta.[1] Perhaps it was in 1862 when he was wounded and sent home from Richmond to recuperate. Possibly like other rural Georgians, he thought his family would be safer in the city. Thus it was to Atlanta that Heck was taken when sent home from the war with typhoid fever.

Atlanta had grown fat and plush on war profits. Population and wealth literally poured into the "Gate City to the South." It ranked number one as a military and commercial depot.[2] In the summer of 1864, General Sherman began his almost superhuman march to the sea, starting at Franklin, Tennessee, and sweeping southward toward Atlanta, a coveted prize for the North.

Heck's brother, Col. Bud Thomas, and the 42nd Georgia Regiment gradually withdrew before Sherman's army. While on a three-day leave of absence to visit his wife and babies at Grandfather Samuel Lee's place, Bud was captured by General Kilpatrick's cavalry, but he managed to escape and rejoined his command.

The Federal troops continued their march to Atlanta, destroying everything in their path. The Confederate soldiers fell back before him. The battles in defense of the city followed in quick succession. The first of these occurred on July 20, 1864.

Driven back, on the night of July 21, the Confederate army shifted its position, fronting Peachtree Creek, and formed a line of battle around the city. In the army's movements around Atlanta the next morning, the 42nd Georgia Regiment, under the command of Colonel Thomas, was put into the battle. All day, the fight centered upon the capture of the DeGress Battery, which was pouring deadly fire upon the grey line. Late that evening, Thomas led his troops a mile and a half through whistling shells and minnie balls until Sherman's men broke. Fighting hand to hand, the 42nd Regiment captured the battery.

Margaret Mitchel immortalized the Battle of Peachtree Creek, in her novel *Gone With the Wind*. When it occurred, Heck, now fourteen-years-old, watched it from afar. Years later, he recalled the battle this way:[3]

> I was returning from a light dinner at a small store on Marietta street when my attention was attracted to a confederate officer on horseback near where the old union depot now stands.
>
> Aides were dashing up to him and away from him, and just at that instant the fight was on at Peach Tree creek, for we could hear the firing and the yelling—that old rebel yell getting fainter and fainter—and we knew the yanks were being driven back.
>
> As I went home that night, I passed an ambulance in which was the body of Gen. Walker, who had been killed that day.
>
> Shortly after dark Bud rode in and told pa, Brother Joe Porter and I to go get what valuables we could haul,

and to get down to Newton county at once—to save what we could, as Atlanta was going to fall. He told us that Gen. Hood was a fighter all right, but that Atlanta was doomed. Bud told us that he led the charge on the yank's breastworks, but that he thought one man had beat him to the works a little.

Atlanta fell on the 28th of July, with a loss of 31,687 Union lives and 34,979 Confederates.[4] The Union forces sacked and burned the city. Most of the inhabitants, including Heck and his family, fled, mourning the violent death of kin and friends.

Immediate survival became the problem. Food and much needed medicines were hard to find, and harder still to buy with inflated Confederate currency. Union troops remained in Atlanta four months, foraging and raiding far into the country to supply their troops. Bacon sold for five dollars a pound; flour a dollar and a half a pound; syrup twenty dollars a gallon; eggs six dollars a dozen; and potatoes and meal twenty dollars a bushel.[5]

When the Union soldiers left Atlanta in mid-November, Heck and his family, along with the other Atlantans, drifted back into the city, picking their way over the burned-out ruins. They shivered at the sight of the fire-blackened chimneys and tombstones where homes and businesses had once stood.

That winter of 1864 was one of the coldest and wettest in Atlanta's memory. Cut by heavy war transports, city streets were muddy and almost impassable. Heck heard the howls of hungry dogs filling the black nights. Looting by half-starved people was prevalent.

On 18 April 1865, General Sherman and General Johnston agreed to a truce and the war ended. Pen Bedell died in fighting in Southern Georgia during the last days of the war, reportedly after the truce was called. Col. Bud Thomas arranged for the comfort and transportation of his men to their various homes. He paid each one, officers and privates alike, a Mexican silver dollar, and bid them a sad farewell. He returned home to find he had lost everything.

Heck's father, Lovick, was never well following the war. Like Bud, he had lost almost everything too. He returned to Atlanta to build a home there and open a small store.

Slowly, Atlanta began to rebuild. Freed Negroes filled the streets, many of them belligerent. Federal soldiers and carpetbaggers moved in. One day when Heck was fifteen, he sat idly outside his father's nearly empty store, wearing a hat made of rabbit fur. Two drunken federal soldiers came by, and one of them snatched his hat and tore it up. In an instant, Heck was up and flying into the man, fists pounding. Lovick appeared in the doorway behind his son, brandishing a hatchet. The second soldier pulled his pistol. Heck leaped upon him. Lovick pulled him off, and took the gun from the man. The soldier jumped to his feet, and the two men fled in terror from the fighting Thomases.[6]

During these years of the Reconstruction period, Heck attended Emory College. Most likely he began studying for the ministry at this time. He developed a fondness for the arts, too, especially poetry. Many years later, he could still quote whole stanzas of "Omar."

It was while in school that Henry A. Thomas received his nickname, "Heck," from a classmate, Charley Clinton.[7] It was by this name he was to go down in history.

In 1867, Heck's father, Lovick Thomas, became chief of police of Atlanta. At the age of seventeen, Heck joined him there, the youngest man on the Atlanta police force.

Those days were a time of intense racial feeling. Excited by the agitations of the Northern carpetbaggers, the Negroes were easily aroused to violence. This culminated in the infamous Bush Arbor Riot shortly after Heck joined the police force.

According to Heck, the fight began when he and a fellow officer, Jack Smith, "arrested a democratic Negro, Andy Whitaker," who "used to be a slave and belonged to Jared I. Whitaker, one of Atlanta's first and best editors."[8]

The Atlanta *Constitution* reported Heck and Smith were on their way to the station house with Whitaker when they "ran into a torchlight procession of radical Negroes." The gang assaulted them and demanded the release of their prisoner.

"The battle was on right then and there . . . and I think I started it," Heck said.[9]

Six other officers hurried to their assistance. They fought under a gaslight on Decatur Street. "A little Negro—he wasn't much bigger than my fist—ran up on my right side and shot me square through the right thigh," Heck told a newspaper reporter. "But I never fell and stayed through the fight."

Though Heck's account of the fight sounded modest, others praised his bravery during the ruckus. They told how the youthful officer kept to his feet, though beaten with clubs, blowing his whistle for help. When shot, he went down with a bullet in his right arm and another in his right thigh. Propped on his elbow, he continued firing into the advancing rioters until they turned and ran.[10]

During the remainder of Heck's time on the Atlanta police force, his reputation as a brave and fearless officer continued to grow.

In 1870, Heck's mother died. The following year, he married his cousin, Isabelle Gray. "Belle" was the daughter of Rev. Albert Gray, a prominent Oxford minister. During the first two years of their marriage, Heck and Belle boarded at the Campbell House, a small hotel at the corner of Decatur and Ivy Streets. Perhaps because Belle considered the police force too dangerous, Heck accepted a job as a clerk for the wholesale grocery firm of A.C. and B.F. Wylie.[11] On 16 December 1872, the couple's first child, Henry Gray Thomas, was born at the Oxford home of Reverend Gray.

By now, Heck had become a well-polished and educated gentleman. Along with his father and brother, Bud, who had also opened a store in Atlanta, Heck held a position of esteem in the city. He and Belle attended Trinity Methodist Church, where Heck sang in his beautiful tenor voice. His Sunday School teacher was Robert A. Hemphill, founder of the Atlanta *Constitution*, whom Heck always recalled as being a great Christian. Hemphill encouraged him in his ambition to become a minister.[12]

But one day, Heck learned that the pastor of Trinity Methodist and a lady had committed adultery. Disillusioned, he gave up his ministry plans and seldom went to church after that. But he never forgot the concepts of Christian virtue that he learned there. Through the remainder of his life, he was to be known as a man of high moral character and honesty.

This is well substantiated in a statement made by June G. Oglesby, a well-known Atlanta wholesale grocery merchant in a letter of reference: "I knew Heck Thomas mighty well, and while I have always considered him as one of the bravest men I have ever known, a man absolutely devoid of fear, I never knew him to be in the least unkind. Like all brave men, he is as gentle and kind as a woman. He would make any sacrifice in his power for a friend, and is ever ready to give his help and assistance to the weak and needy."[13]

Even so, Heck knew something was missing from his life. With this reference, he began to look for new opportunity.

In 1871, Heck Thomas worked as a receiving and shipping clerk for a large wholesale grocery firm in Atlanta. Courtesy Thomas Collection.

Chapter 4

Express Messenger on the Texas Frontier

In 1873, Heck Thomas eyed the bustling frontier of Texas. It stood on the edge of the rapidly expanding West. Farms were being settled and towns springing up. Railroad magnates raced to push their lines westward to California. To the north of Texas, lay the prohibited Indian Territory. That whole country sounded the call of adventure to Heck. He developed what he called "a severe case of Texas fever, and left the red hills of Georgia for the broad prairies of Texas."[1]

Exactly where he went on that first trip to the Lone Star State is uncertain. Most likely it was to Galveston where his cousin, James L. "Jim" Thomas had obtained a job as a messenger with the Texas Express Company. What is certain is that Heck liked what he saw in Texas. But Belle was a cultured lady, and the harsh aspect of frontier life did not appeal to her as a place for raising children. So Heck returned unwillingly to Georgia.

During the next two years, Heck continued working as a shipping and receiving clerk for the wholesale grocery firm of A.C. and B.F. Wylie. He and Belle lived on Tatnall Street

(Trebursey Street). Their second child, Belle Fullwood Thomas, was born on July 15, 1875, with Belle returning to the home of her father in Oxford for the occasion.

But Heck could not forget the "broad prairies of Texas," and the vast opportunities for an adventurous spirit such as his. Cousin Jim urged him to join him there. Heck pleaded with Belle time and again to go west with him, she kept saying no. Finally, Heck could stand it no longer. He said he was going regardless. His friends and Belle tried to talk him out of it, but he would not be swayed. In preparation, he obtained a second letter of recommendation which was willingly given:[2]

> Atlanta, Ga.   Ap. 8, 1876
>
> This will introduce to you our young friend Henry A. Thomas, and it gives us pleasure to say a good word for him. He visits your state with a view of making it his home, leaving many warm friends behind. He has been connected with one of the largest wholesale grocery houses in the state for seven years. As a receiving and shipping clerk and filled this important position with great satisfaction to his employers. He is quick, industrious affable and the best of all, honest. And the best wishes of the business men of this city goes with him.
>
> Benjamin E. Crane,
> President, Atlanta
> Chamber of Commerce

Nine other prominent Atlanta men added their signatures to that of Crane's.

With his two letters of recommendation in hand, Heck was sure he would have no trouble obtaining a job in Texas. Seeing that her husband was fully determined to go west, willingly or not, Belle gave in. When the young couple and their family arrived on a boat, they found Galveston was a bustling seaport town with tall-masted schooners in the harbor. Immigrants poured through the city, riding the trains with their heavy bundles, or plodding behind cumbersome wagons. With his letters of recommendation, Heck quickly obtained a job with the Texas Express Company, which had its headquarters in Houston.

Heck recorded his impressions of the company years later: "There are many railroads now that of course were not thought of in Texas at that time, but there was only one Express Company in the whole broad state. This was the 'Texas Express Company.' It was afterwards opposed by the Pacific Express Company and by the Wells, Fargo Express. The Texas was an offspring of the Southern Express, but as the Southern Express was a Georgia Company and the Pacific Express was Jay Gould's company and as that company was on its own lines, the Texas Express only lasted a few years after they began working against this full company."[3]

Heck was assigned as a messenger on the Galveston to Denison run. In Denison, north of Dallas and Fort Worth near Indian Territory, many families still resided in tents. Indian scares were frequent. The McKinney Road near Denison and Dallas was daily whitened with long lines of covered wagons. A roundhouse was being built at Denison. The Fort Worth depot had not been "located" yet, but the railroads were steadily pushing west, fed by large grants of public land. For a time, things went quietly for Heck, but one day, a fellow by the name of Sam Bass opened the biggest season of train robbery Texas was to ever know, and initiated Heck proper into the ways of outlaws.

Sam Bass had been born in Indiana in 1851, so was only a year older than Heck. Orphaned and reared by an uncle,

Bass began to drift early in life. On the Mississippi, he became skilled with a gun and as a card sharp. He went to Texas and for a time handled horses for Sheriff "Dad" Egan at Denton. Gaining a sorrel horse known as "the Denton mare," Bass soon won enough racing the mare to leave Egan. Bass chipped in with Joel Collins on a cattle herd and trailed it north. In the Black Hills of South Dakota, the two ventured into the freighting business, then a saloon, and finally purchased a mine. Here they went broke. To recoup their losses, they robbed seven stages. They learned large shipments of gold were being sent over the Union Pacific. Organizing a gang, on September 10, 1877, they robbed a train at Big Spring, Nebraska, of sixty thousand dollars.

The gang separated. Several were caught. Bass made it safely back to Denton. He flashed around more money than he had ever been known to have before. His money was soon gone. In the spring of 1878, Bass organized a new gang, including a thirty-year-old whiskered individual with glasses. The gang established several hideouts in the "Cross Timbers," a tangled belt of small postoak and blackjack east of Denton. The belt ranged from five to thirty miles wide and extended from the Arkansas River southwestward to the Brazos River, a distance of about four hundred miles.

The Bass gang struck first on February 22, 1878, at the Allen station on the Houston and Texas Central, eight miles south of McKinney. Cousin Jim Thomas was the Texas Express messenger on that run.

The train had left Denison an hour late that evening. Jim was calmly going about his business when he heard the words: "Throw up your hands and give us your money."[4]

Jim glanced up. He saw four masked men at the door. Drawing quickly, he fired on the men. They retreated. Jim entrenched himself behind some equipment. He exchanged more shots with the robbers, wounding one in the wrist. The robbers disconnected the express car and had the engineer move it fifty to one hundred feet from the rest of the train. The robbers threatened to burn Jim out. Seeing little else he could do, he gave up.

With a gun held to his head, he unlocked the express safe. The robbers took six or seven packages containing about fifteen hundred dollars from the safe. They fled in a westerly direction. The train was full, carrying 175 passengers. But reportedly, none carried a gun to give chase.

At the end of the run in Galveston, the messengers had a room where they made out their reports and waited for their next trip. A number of men gathered there, including Heck. They listened with interest as Jim related his experience. "I would not have given up if I could have gotten to my cartridge box," Jim said. "But I only had one cartridge left when I quit."

Heck did not doubt his cousin's courage, but he said if the same thing happened to him, he would not let the robbers get the money.

"What would you do?" Jim challenged.

"I don't know," Heck said, "but I'd think of something."

The day after the robbery, Chief Agent W. K. Cornish of the Texas Express arrived in Dallas. With him were Jim Thomas and Heck. They had been given leave and a special commission to ride with Cornish in search of the robbers, Jim to make identity and Heck for protection because of his law enforcement training.[5]

The three went immediately to Allen Station. A local saloon keeper remembered that Tom Spotswood, a farmer who lived fifteen miles northeast of Allen, had been in town inquiring about the train shortly before its arrival. Spotswood seemed to fit Jim's description of one of the robbers. Riding out to see Spotswood, Jim identified him. Cornish arrested the farmer and jailed him in McKinney.

The three detectives continued their search for the other robbers. In the heavy bottoms of the rugged Cross Timbers, they had no luck. Heck and Jim returned to their messenger jobs after two weeks.

Heck realized his express car might be held up next. He laid plans as to what he would do if this should occur. He did not have long to wait before he got a chance to put those plans into action and was wounded again in the process. What happened that day has been much told and glorified in tales of the Old West. But Heck told it modestly:[6]

> On the night of March 18, 1878, while I was running as express messenger for this company the train was held up at Hutchins, Tex. The express car and engine were run 400 yds. down the track, the engineer, fireman, railroad agent and others forced to stand in front of the express car door to keep the messenger from firing on the robbers. The door was smashed in with an ax. The robbers has [sic] been firing through the car and I was shot twice, one entering the neck and the other under the left eye. I had previously fixed up some decoy packages and put them in my safe, fixing them up to look like regular money packages. This I had done as there had been a number of train robberies through the country. I think I was shot by conductor or brakeman.*

---

*Heck Thomas scratched out this last sentence in his handwritten account of the affair. It may have been true according to related stories in the Galveston *Daily News*. It was in this first blast of buckshot that Heck was wounded. The scar beneath his eye was scarcely visible in later years.

> When I saw the robbers as the train pulled into the station, I took the money packages containing some $22,000 from the safe and hid it in the ashes of the stove leaving a small sack of silver some $89.00, and the decoy packages in the safe there as the outlaws were building a fire under my car to roast me, let them enter the car. I was forced to unlock the safe and throw the silver and decoy packages in the sack that the leader held open. The conductor and brakeman in the meantime had slipped from the back of the train, run across to a hotel and borrowed a shotgun, but had no ammunition and ran to a hardware store to procure some after which they slipped back to the train opening fire in the robber gang. But as he had only buck shot did not do much damage. The robbers were gradually making their way to their horses and vaulting to their saddles disappeared in the night."

Heck's modest tale left out the details of his own heroism. The Galveston *Daily News* was quick to provide them for hungry readers. It reported that on first seeing the bandits with their hostages, Heck had slammed the door shut and refused to open it though the bandits were firing into the car and hacking at the door with an axe. Afterwards, though wounded and his own gun taken by the outlaws, Heck obtained another weapon and joined the fight against the bandits. The men exchanged thirty to forty shots. Heck got to the engineer and told him to forget the fight, that he had the money safe and to get the train out of there before the bandits discovered his ruse. Heck tied up his wounds as best he could, and insisted on completing his run. But at Corsicana, he had to stop and see a doctor.[7] He could never see as well out of his left eye after that.

Heck arrived in Galveston the following day on the 1:35 p.m. train. Before going home to Belle on Eighth Street and Mechanic or seeking further medical treatment, he rendered his usual account of his business. In the back room, Cousin Jim and their fellow messengers besieged Heck for information. Jim and Heck compared the two robberies. It wasn't long before the two men realized the robbers of both trains had been the Sam Bass gang.

Wild excitement raced across the frontier at this news. Texas was accustomed to crime, but wholesale train robbery was unknown. Bankers and storekeepers placed loaded guns against the walls in their establishments within easy reach. Reporters swarmed into Dallas and Denton County, seeking the most exciting news since General Lee's surrender.[8]

Heck recovered rapidly from his wounds.[9] He found himself being called a hero for outwitting the robbers, and received the following citation of appreciation:[10]

Houston, Texas, Mar. 22, 1878

Henry A. Thomas Esq., Messenger H. & T. C. Route.

Dear Sir:

Enclosed please find the sum of two hundred dollars, which I hand to you in the name of the Texas Express Co. and beg your acceptance thereof as a slight recognition of the zeal and fidelity displayed by you in the robbery of this company at Hutchins on the night of March 18, 1878. The officials of this company realize the fact that your coolness, foresight and thoughtfulness were instruments in thwarting the designs of the robbers, and reducing to a minimum the amount of booty secured by them, and were it not for the extreme depression of business and the serious losses lately sustained, they would testify in a more substantial manner to their high appreciation of your conduct which has stamped you in the estimation of the officers of this company as in all respects a first class messenger.

Trusting that your fellow messengers will be encouraged to emulate your example should this occasion again arise.

> I am respectfully,
> C. T. Campbell,
> Superintendent

Heck and Jim each received a gold watch from the company. As a further reward, Heck was promoted to express agent at Fort Worth, a job he was to hold for seven years.

But the other messengers proved not so brave as Campbell had hoped. The Sam Bass gang struck again on April 5 at Eagle Ford, six miles west of Dallas. Five days later, they robbed the express at Mesquite, twelve miles east of Dallas. Express men Hickox and Gross were discharged from service for "nonresistance to the robbers."[11]

The offer of fifteen hundred dollars reward for each of the robbers drew an estimated one hundred and fifty Sam Bass hunters into the area.[12] Citizens locked their doors and demanded protection against the desperados.

Major Jones of the Texas Rangers was called to the scene as there was no ranger company in the area. Jones organized a detachment in Dallas as part of Company B.[13] City Recorder Junis "June" Peak, a former deputy sheriff and city marshal, was sworn in as captain.

Peak and his men trailed the Sam Bass gang for several months. They finally ran them to ground at Round Rock north of Austin, July 20, 1878. Bass was shot and killed and his gang scattered. The excitement died down.

Heck moved his family to Fort Worth and settled into his new job as express agent. Fort Worth in those days was a typical rough, frontier town. Cowboys regularly rode in from the trail herds on their way to Denison, looking for entertainment. The inevitable riffraff followed them. Vice seemed virtually unchecked. In the first three years of Fort Worth's organized government, which had begun in 1873, the city had one city marshal and four police chiefs. The last chief of police had remained but three months.[14] Belle hated the thought of moving to Fort Worth with its wild, uncouth people even more than she had the Texas coast.

Heck, however, seemed to thrive on this type of atmosphere. It reminded him of Reconstruction days in Atlanta. In 1877, a new city marshal, Jim Courtright, had taken over and made considerable headway in cleaning up Fort Worth. After Heck's arrival, he and Courtright became friends and Heck learned much about law enforcement from him.

While in Fort Worth, Heck and Belle became the parents of two more children. Albert was born on August 11, 1879, and Mary Joe on December 22, 1883.

Competition had been increasing for the Texas Express Company and they continued experiencing financial difficulties. In September 1884, the company cut employee wages twelve and one-half percent. Coal chute and freight house men were getting only one dollar and fifteen cents a day. Those on the runs, including Heck, were forced to pay the company fifteen dollars a month for boarding expenses.

On February 23, 1885, the Houston & Texas Central Railway Company failed and went into receivership.[15] March 5, a large group of railroad employees met at Denison and agreed to strike until wages were raised.[16] The strike spread rapidly. A number of employees were fired because of their refusal to work. The strike continued until March 16 when it was settled.

After the strike, it was obvious to Heck that the Texas Express Co. would not last much longer. He decided he needed to look for another job. He was tired of being an express agent and considered it not much better than a receiving and shipping clerk in Atlanta. His friend Jim Courtwright urged him to run for city marshal.

Taking leave of absence from Texas Express, Heck ran for city marshal of Fort Worth on April 8, 1885. The Galveston *Daily News* reported it was, "One of the most hotly contested elections ever held in the city . . . ."[17]

Several fights occurred near the polling places. The judges became excited and closed the polling places nine minutes early. Heck had forty-one of his own men standing in line at the time to cast their ballots. He lost the election by twenty-nine votes. Courtwright and Heck's other friends expressed their bitterness over his defeat.[18]

Heck was disappointed, too, and his appetite was whetted to get back into law enforcement. In early May, he opened the Fort Worth Detective Association. Among his first customers was Alva Roff, a wealthy rancher from the Delaware Bend country on the Red River north of Denton.[19]

Roff handed Heck a "wanted" poster which named Jim and Pink Lee for cattle stealing. The Lee brothers headed a gang which was terrorizing northern Texas and southern Indian Territory. The Lees had killed four men during a recent arrest attempt, including a U.S. deputy marshal and two of Roff's brothers, Jim and Andy. Roff informed Heck he was offering a reward of twenty-five hundred dollars each for Jim and Pink Lee. The state of Texas had added another one thousand dollars. The reward was to be paid on delivery at the jail, dead or alive. Tempted, Heck promised to consider Roff's offer, though he knew it was a dangerous undertaking.

At this time, the territory north of the Red River was an unknown land except to the Indians, cattlemen with grazing permits, outlaws, and U.S. deputy marshals who tried to keep the federal law there. The Indian Nations had their own tribal laws and policed their lands with what they called the Light Horse. Indian laws did not apply to white men. The only way a white man could remain in the territory was to marry an Indian. But Pink and Jim Lee had done just that. To arrest the Lees in Chickasaw country meant that the arresting officers could be hunted down by both Indian and outlaw friends of the two bandits before the officers could cross the Red River into Texas. Heck had no authority in Indian Territory. For a time he delayed taking action. But after several posses were sent after the Jim and Pink Lee gang and failed, he determined to give the capture of the gang a try.

He set off alone on June 5. At Whitesboro, he picked up a friend, Jim Taylor, whom he had met while chasing the Sam Bass gang. Taylor held a U.S. deputy marshal's commission in the Chickasaw Nation. Heck explained his plan to Taylor. Instead of capturing the Lees in Indian Territory, they would try to flush them into Texas where they had no friends to protect them. Then they would capture them. The idea sounded good to Taylor; the large reward made it worthwhile. The two men loaded up and set off for the Nations, prepared for a long stay.

"It was a long and hazardous chase," Heck said later.[20] "Sick and disheartened at times, I resolved I would get them."

He finally "obliterated the gang." The Galveston *Daily News* detailed the story:[21]

> Gainesville - September 8 - Last night, about 12 o'clock, a wagon arrived in the city carrying the dead bodies of Jim and Pink Lee, the noted desperadoes, who have for several months been a terror to the people of Delaware Bend, a part of the Indian Territory.

> This morning an inquest was held and the following facts were gathered:
>
> Heck Thomas, a detective from Fort Worth, Jim Taylor and Jim Sattles, of this county, learned yesterday that the Lee boys were in the Washington neighborhood, near Dexter, about 3 o'clock in the afternoon and officers found the Lees cutting John Washington's pasture fence. The officers crept up to within 40 yards and ordered the men to surrender, but were fired on for answer. They returned the fire, killing Pink Lee and shooting Jim through the neck at the first volley. Jim Lee fired about 10 shots before he died and the officials kept up the shooting until he ceased, though only two shots struck him.
>
> They were brought here in order to get the reward of $2,000 offered by citizens.
>
> All day a large crowd of curious people have been around the courthouse looking at the bodies. They were brave and determined men, but their looks show them to have been ignorant and brutal. This disposes of the last of the gang, the others being in jail at Fort Worth.

"The day I got these men," Heck added, "they were riding a couple of stolen horses and had robbed and burned a ranch house just a few days before."[22]

"I weighed 171 lbs. the day I started on this campaign, the day it ended I was down to 132 lbs.

"That whole part of the country breathed easier to know they were dead . . . ."

Governor John Ireland declared Heck's feat "one of the most remarkable in the history of Texas Law enforcement."[23]

Heck returned home to find he was being hailed as a hero again. Fort Worth prepared a "royal reception" for him, feeling "justly proud of his bravery."[24]

Even more important, Heck knew he had found his life's work. When in the Nations chasing the outlaws, he had seen a real need for brave officers there. He expressed his desire for a U.S. deputy marshal's commission in Indian Territory. Belle voiced objections, but Heck had made up his mind. Deciding he didn't want to go back to work for Texas Express, and shunning offers to run for sheriff on the Democrat ticket in Tarrant County and an appointment with the Texas Rangers, with the encouragement of his friend, Jim Taylor, he sat down and wrote out his application to the U.S. marshal at Fort Smith.

Chapter 5

U. S. Deputy Marshal in Indian Territory

During the late 1800s, the jurisdiction of the Western District of the Federal Court extended across parts of Arkansas and Texas as well as Indian Territory. Indian Territory (present Oklahoma) was considered a "maelstrom of racial hatred, rape, robbery and murder."[1] The Federal Court in Fort Smith was corrupted by ineffective officers and bribery.

In 1875, President Grant appointed Isaac C. Parker as judge of the Fort Smith court. Under Parker's stern, legalistic hand much of the corruption there ended. Judge Parker sat on the bench for fourteen years. His was the largest criminal court in the United States. It held "original, final and exclusive jurisdiction with no appeal, unique in legal history."[2]

Judge Parker presided over four terms a year, but in truth, they were as one.[3] Court continued throughout the year and Parker dispatched business with uncommon speed for a Federal judge. He became known as "The Hanging Judge," condemning eighty-seven men to death. The court's executioner, George Maledon, gained notoriety as "The Prince of Hangmen."

Even so, Parker stood as a pillar of justice in a wild and untamed land. Throughout his life, Heck held a great deal of respect for Judge Parker. He called him a "fine man, a Christian man." Portly in appearance, Parker had white hair with a matching goatee and mustache and kind blue eyes. It was said that he cried after sentencing men to death, and on hanging days, he prayed at home for the condemned men.[4]

The U.S. marshal's office maintained a staff of twenty-five to fifty deputies and "posse without number" for bringing in law breakers. Most of these came from Indian Territory. Those arrested there could be charged only with Federal offenses such as introducing and selling liquor, larceny, murder, rape, adultery, and postal violations. Twenty-four to forty violators a week were brought in and examined and released or bound over for trial.

In general, twenty to forty prisoners charged with murder awaited trial at all times. Five to twenty men were hung each year. Hundreds of prisoners, thousands of witnesses, juries, and hordes of lawyers, all in constant attendance, required a large outlay of money by the court.[5] Sometimes the court had to recess for several months because Congress had not appropriated enough funds to keep it in business.[6]

In Indian Territory, the Indians had their own tribunals and law officers. Parker's court held jurisdiction only over white citizens. Twenty to thirty deputy marshals patrolled the seventy-four thousand square miles in Indian Territory.

Sometimes it seemed to Heck that all the outlaws in the nation were hiding in the Territory. Few decent men wanted to risk their lives going into the lawless land. Often those who did were shot by friends of those whom they tried to arrest. Records indicate that sixty-five officers died in the line of duty during Judge Parker's reign and dozens more were wounded.[7]

The Federal Court of the Western District of Arkansas in Fort Smith. The infamous jail, feared by all prisoners, was located in the basement. **Photo by Bonnie Speer.**

Judge Issac C. Parker was appointed Federal Judge of the Fort Smith Court May 10, 1876, by President Grant. He served until his death, Nov. 17, 1896, sending eighty-eight men to the scaffold during his term. **Courtesy Western History Collections, University of Oklahoma Library.**

When submitting his application to the Western District of the Federal Court in Fort Smith, Heck well knew that deputy marshals received no salary, only fees and mileage. Fees consisted of fifty cents for serving papers, two dollars for an arrest, and a dollar a day expense money while chasing a person for whom he held a warrant, providing he could turn in receipts for his expenditures. Also, the deputy was allowed seventy-five cents a day to feed each prisoner. Expenses such as paying for information, hiring a posse or guards came out of the deputy's own pocket.[8]

Mileage allowance was six cents a mile while on official business: ten cents for the deputy marshal and his prisoner—if he brought in his man. If he killed his man, he got nothing, and even forfeited his dollar a day expense money prior to the killing.

Heck knew a deputy couldn't collect any of the rewards offered by the government as that was part of the job he was hired to do. Sometimes, the rewards offered by individuals and even companies could not be collected. All told the deputies were lucky if they made five hundred dollars a year. Still, Heck reasoned, a deputy could do all right if he could pick up a few rewards.

Heck obtained his first commission in the Western District of the Federal Court under Deputy Marshal Thomas Boles. On January 8, 1886, he brought in his first prisoners to the court. Four of them were charged with larceny and one with assault.[9] Heck shoved the five men in among the other one hundred and thirty prisoners crowding the damp, dark, two-room basement jail beneath Parker's courtroom, and set off to seek more lawbreakers.[10]

Shortly after Heck's arrival in Fort Smith, Grover Cleveland was elected President of the United States. Cleveland replaced Boles, a Republican, with John Carroll, a Democrat. As was the custom, the incoming marshal called all the deputies in to see which ones he would keep and let go.

Many of the men who volunteered as deputy marshals were as lawless as the men they sought. Inefficient and brutal, some had the habit of letting their prisoners escape if more money could be made this way instead of taking their prisoners to jail.[11] Others had a dominate trait for drinking whiskey and a lack of scruples about taking human life.[12]

The Fort Smith *Elevator* expressed its hope that Marshal Carroll would discard the "uncouth and brutal officers whose most predominate characteristic is the capacity for taking human life" and the "lawless cutthroats who have been making a hell upon earth of this country for so long a time," and to "appoint gentlemen as deputies . . . men who have some regard for life and property of the people with whom they are brought in contact."[13]

Heck seemed made to order in that respect. Marshal Carroll retained him on his staff of deputies. Perhaps being a Democrat and a Confederate like Marshal Carroll helped Heck also.

None of the deputy marshals worked harder to rid Indian Territory of its desperate criminals than Heck Thomas. Tireless, he rode all over the area, searching out the worst type of border ruffians and cutthroats. Bill Tilghman, Heck's fellow deputy marshal in Oklahoma Territory, once suggested Heck was a little foolhardy and rushed in sometimes when he should have waited. Even so, stories about Heck's bravery and valor began to mount. Few issues of the Fort Smith *Elevator* failed to mention his name. On January 26, 1887, the paper headlined its story: "HECK THOMAS BRINGS IN 12 PRISONERS - One of the Most Active Officers in the Western District."

The article went on to say, "Deputy Heck Thomas was out 52 days, and his trip is classed as the best one made by any officer for many a day." His "brag capture" was Della Humby, a murderer who had been with the Jim and Pink Lee gang. Being in the Chickasaw Nation, Heck had heard Humby was nearby. He trailed the outlaw eleven days, and caught up with him in the Seminole Nation, "taking him unawares."

Heck left Fort Smith again on February 25 for the Chickasaw country on another roundup. "He expects to be out 40 to 50 days," noted the *Elevator*. "Criminals in that locality had better begin hunting their holes."[14]

Soon Heck's name was feared by outlaws all over Indian Territory. He consistently brought in more prisoners than any other deputy. On November 21, 1887, he set a record for a single trip, bringing in forty-one prisoners. With the help of his guards, he had hauled them in seven two-horse wagons a distance of 275 miles. On December 2 of that year, Heck returned to the Fort Smith jail with thirty-two prisoners. He came in again on December 16 with thirty-eight prisoners. Twelve of them were charged with murder.

Traveling overland, the deputies shackled their prisoners to trees or to their wagons. When they struck camp near town, curious citizens crowded around.[15] Guards were stationed near the prisoners. Drivers carried no guns in case the prisoners should get ideas. When herding the prisoners through the settlements, guards always kept careful watch lest friends of the prisoners take exception to their arrest.

The deputies were out in all kinds of weather. It took them several weeks to make the long trip to Fort Smith. By now, railroads were being built into Indian Territory. Heck suggested to the authorities in Fort Smith and Washington that it would be less expensive for the deputies to haul their prisoners by trains. This would also save time and be less dangerous for the lawmen. At the time nothing was done, but later, the government did start using railroads to transport federal prisoners.[16]

As Heck rode along the trail while man hunting, he kept notes of his daily activities in one of his pocket-size, leather-bound "day books." The Thomas family still has most of these day books. Heck had beautiful handwriting. On page after page he recorded notes about the outlaws he was chasing, his travels, expenses, descriptions of wanted men, and names of witnesses. Occasionally he inserted a family note. Once he made a cryptic comment about the weather: "Whew, it's cold!"

In one of the small books is a recipe for hair dye. His daughter, Beth, said she had no idea why her father wanted that. In another day book, Heck wrote down a cure for the "blind staggers." This certainly would have been useful if one of his horses had gotten into a corn patch or grain bin and overeaten.

Many notes in Heck's day books attest to one of the biggest problems in the Territory "introducing and selling" whiskey. Legitimate whiskey sellers operated in the saloons in the Territory, but dozens of others ran stills and sold whiskey illegally to the Indians. Often, the whiskey runners were more dangerous than murderers when apprehended.

The Fort Smith *Elevator* noted that in the federal court, "Ninety-five percent of the criminal matter presented is directly traceable to liquor."[17] The editor expressed his awareness of the diligence of the marshals, but believed their job too hazardous, and that there was not enough staff for suppression of the illegal whiskey trade. "Without whiskey and weapons," he said, "the Indian problem would be solved."

Heck never mistreated a prisoner, nor allowed his men to do so. Nor did he ever shoot anybody that he didn't have to. He said he always gave the man a chance to give up first.

Once Heck captured a gang of cattle thieves and murderers that thrived near Southwest City, Missouri. In appreciation, the citizens of that town presented him with an engraved saddle.

With his long hard hours in the saddle, Heck developed into peak physical condition. A large man, he stood about six-feet tall, with wide shoulders and narrow hips. As a Texas Express messenger, he had worn a thick black beard. Now he sported a rather long mustache which shaded his firm mouth. Naturally dark complexioned, his skin became even darker from being outdoors so much.

Even on the trail, Heck managed to maintain a semblance of being well dressed. He never forgot his manners and retained his soft, Southern drawl.

"Heck Thomas was one of the finest specimens of physical manhood one would want to see," one writer once commented.[18] "He was one of those dashing, intrepid officers who was always alert; of undaunted courage and who attracted the most daredevil young men in the country as his possemen. He and his men were always mounted and equipped on the best horses and with the finest arms of the day; and to see him in the field was a sight never to be forgotten."

By 1887, Fort Smith had grown considerably. It had eight hundred new homes with gas and electric lights and telephones within forty miles. Two railroads, the Valley Route of the Missouri Pacific, and South Western Branch of the St. Louis and San Francisco served the city.[19] For a time after Heck joined the U.S. marshal's force, he and his family lived in a hotel room in Fort Smith. Then Heck found a small house to rent. Belle didn't like living here any better than she did in Fort Worth, though admittedly Fort Smith was more refined than the Texas cow town. Who could blame her, being cooped up with a passel of children among strangers? Her husband was gone much of the time, and knowing Marshal Carroll had lost nine deputies, two possemen, and three guards since the first of the year couldn't have helped Belle's feelings either.

Belle's brother, Rev. Albert Gray, had married Heck's aunt, Pamelia Thomas, and was now a Methodist missionary serving as principal at New Hope Seminary, a Choctaw school located near Spiro in Indian Territory. Belle visited with her brother occasionally. Even so, she still felt isolated and longed for Georgia and the Southern culture in which she had been reared and where she wanted to rear her children.

On April 22, 1886, Congress had established two new Federal courts with jurisdiction in the northern part of Texas and part of the Choctaw Nation in Indian Territory. The first of these was at Paris, Texas, with control over Lamar, Fanin, Red River, and Della Counties, and all of the southern part of the Choctaw Nation. The second court ruled over Grayson County, Texas, and part of the Choctaw Nation.[20] Heck was commissioned in the Paris court as well as that in Fort Smith. In early 1888, he moved his family to White Bead Hill, in the Chickasaw Nation, just west of the Choctaw Nation.

If Belle felt isolated in Fort Smith, she must have felt even more so here. The coming of the railroad to nearby Paul's Valley had bypassed White Bead Hill and already cast its shadow over it. The day the Thomas family arrived, the town consisted of little more than two hotels, the Thompson and Waite General Merchandise, a livery, and a drug store.

According to the Chickasaw *Enterprise* not much had been happening in the town since the holidays, except for the outlaws and whiskey peddlers, who sometimes brought their depredations right into town, shooting up the place. Dances were a thing of the past. A few select musicals, and several play parties had been presented. The newspaper reported the ladies of White Bead Hill were planning a "riding club" when the cold weather was over.[21]

Possibly White Bead Hill's only saving grace, as far as Belle was concerned, was the Methodist Church pastored by the Reverend Powell, which she could attend, and the Pierce Institute where she could enroll her children in school.[22]

Heck tried to make things a little easier on Belle. In White Bead Hill he rented a house for his family and hired a maid to help Belle with her work. Years later, the son of this woman at White Bead Hill, brought Heck's youngest daughter, Beth, some pictures she had taken of the family then. From her picture, Beth noted that Belle, though no beauty, wasn't a bad looking woman. Tall like her husband, she wore her dark hair piled high on her head.

On August 21, 1887, Belle gave birth to her and Heck's fifth and last child, Lovick Howard Thomas. It wasn't long after this that Belle determined she had all of Indian Territory she could stand. She begged Heck to return to Georgia with her. She considered the Territory too uncivilized and didn't want any more of it. Heck refused to go. He told her he had a job to do here. His father had died in 1878, shortly after Heck had become a U.S. deputy marshal, and he felt there was nothing for him to go back to in Georgia.

One day, as soon as Belle was able to travel, she took the children and went to Georgia. Heck didn't know at the time that they were separating. He received a note from Belle at Christmas saying she had put the children in school there. He wrote suggesting she return at once. She said, "No."

Heck never blamed Belle, according to Beth. But Belle had tried to force him to return to Georgia, and he was not the type one could force. In later years, he told his second wife, Matie, that he and Belle had never got along well. In addition, he admitted man hunting had gotten into his blood.

Heck may have gone back to Georgia to talk to Belle at that time. An undated clipping in the Thomas papers states, "Atlanta Man Going to the Klondike."[23] It told about Heck's plan to get up a party of twenty-five Atlanta men to accompany him in his search for wealth.

But he soon forgot about gold hunting, and returning to Indian Territory, he threw himself back into man hunting. Not long after this, he received the worst wound of his life.

The Aaron and Tom Purdy gang had a still on Snake Creek, sixteen miles south of Red Fork. The gang was also suspected of robbing a train near Catoosa the night of June 15, 1888. Heck and his partner set out to arrest them for "introducing and selling whiskey in the Indian country."[24]

They came upon Aaron Purdy and another of the gang members in the wagon they used to peddle the whiskey. Both men resisted arrest. In the subsequent gun fight, the officers captured Baker, the wagon, horses, and liquor. Purdy escaped on one of the horses in Heck's outfit.[25]

Heck set out on Purdy's trail. On June 26, Heck and his men located the Purdy gang's still in a deep ravine. Heck rode boldly up the ravine in advance of his men. He called for the moonshiners to come out. In response, the Purdy gang opened fire. One of the bullet's struck Heck in the left side, leaving an eight-inch long cut, and another shattered his right wrist. In the volley of gunfire that followed from Heck's men, Aaron Purdy went down badly wounded. The rest of the gang dropped their guns and surrendered.[26]

Both Heck and Purdy were bleeding badly. The weather was quite warm. One of Heck's men rode to an Indian tepee about a mile from the scene of the fight and procured a canteen of water. When he returned, Purdy looked at the water so longingly that Heck told the deputy to give the outlaw the first drink, although he had been shot through the body, too, and the first thing a man in that condition wanted was a drink of water.[27]

Heck stood by as his men loaded the wounded outlaw into the back of a wagon. He rode horseback beside the wagon, sixteen miles to the railroad, holding his left arm to his side where the blood was gushing, and his right hand hanging uselessly.[28]

When he reached Red Fork, Heck found no doctor available there. He rode on to Tulsa, another fifteen miles. By the time he reached the home of Dr. H. P. Newlin, the town's first physician, Heck had lost a lot of blood and was nearly dead.

But that soon proved to be a lucky break for him, for that was where he met his second wife.

Chapter 6

A Storybook Romance

Matie Mowbray had arrived in Tulsa only three months before with her parents, Rev. George and Hannah Mowbray. Reverend Mowbray was a large bearded man with a dour expression. He had been sent to Tulsa as a Methodist missionary when the former pastor was frightened away by a bunch of roughnecks.[1]

The Mowbrays had immigrated to the United States from England. There they could trace their roots back to William the Conqueror and Lord Mowbray of England.[2] First they settled in Elmira, New York. In 1887, Reverend Mowbray obtained a church in McCune, Kansas. In March 1888 he accepted the position as missionary in Indian Territory.

Matie, fifteen, was the third of four children. She and her younger sister, Grace, twelve, accompanied their parents to Tulsa in a jump-seat buggy. The older children, Annie and George, Jr., remained in the States for several months.[3]

Tulsa had been settled on the banks of the Arkansas River in 1872 on the site of a former Indian town in the Creek Nation.[4] The railroad arrived ten years later. Thomas Jefferson "Jeff" Archer, a red-headed, mixed-blood Cherokee, who later married Matie's older sister, Annie, erected the first store building in Tulsa in December 1882.

At the time the Mowbrays arrived, Tulsa had a population of 123 living within a two-mile radius in a collection of shacks.[5] Sanitation was bad. Cattle, horses, and hogs roamed freely in the streets, infesting the shacks with bed bugs. Nearly everyone who came to Tulsa got typhoid fever. The cowboys in the Cherokee Strip came to town on payday and celebrated, getting drunk and riding up and down the streets at breakneck speed, shooting and "goggling," knocking out every light they saw.[6] On Sundays the cowboys fired their pistols over the heads of the church goers. They said they did this, not to frighten the church members, but because it was fun to hear the women scream.[7]

Several outlaw gangs had hideouts near Tulsa. The outlaws stole horses, held up trains, and robbed stores. There was no marshal stationed in Tulsa to keep the peace. Occasionally, a federal deputy, such as Heck Thomas, rode through. It was said that the outlaws always stopped on Stovepipe Hill overlooking Tulsa, to survey the hitching rails to see if the deputy marshal's familiar horse was tied there.[8]

After his arrival in Tulsa, Reverend Mowbray was anxious to increase his Sunday School enrollment in the Methodist Church. He suggested to Matie she start a day school at the church, because, as the Presbyterian Church had already proven, where the children went to mission school, they would go to Sunday School. Matie was only fifteen-years-old, but she had passed a creditable teacher's examination in Pennsylvania at the age of fourteen. She became the second mission schoolteacher in Tulsa.

Though young in years, Matie had the appearance of a fully developed woman. She was best friends with Dr. H.P. Newlin's daughter, whom she visited often. Perchance, she arrived at the Newlin home on June 27, 1888. When invited in, she walked into the dining room. Not knowing anyone else was there, Matie stopped short at sight of the blood-stained, disheveled deputy marshal sitting there.

Dr. Newlin introduced the two. Heck Thomas was weak from his loss of blood following his fight with the Purdy gang. He apologized to Matie for his appearance and not rising in her presence. He could not take his eyes off the slender, brown-haired, green-eyed young woman. Matie in turn was entranced by the bronzed, courtly deputy marshal with the soft Southern drawl.

"I thought he was the handsomest man I had ever seen," Matie romanticized of their meeting years later. "Just my ideal of what a frontier marshal should be."[9]

During the next ten days, while Heck was recuperating with his right hand in a splint, he and Matie had a chance to get well acquainted. Matie had dainty handwriting and was an excellent speller. She volunteered to help write his report on the capture of Aaron Purdy. Thereafter, Heck fondly called her his "little schoolteacher," and she called him "boss" as his guards did.[10]

From the beginning, Matie intrigued Heck. She was attractive, intelligent, and a fine conversationalist. Though not divorced yet, Heck was still unhappy over his situation with Belle. He missed his children. He had asked Belle again to return to Indian Territory and once more she refused. He could not think of returning to Georgia.

At that time, Federal law in Indian Territory automatically granted a divorce upon application to a Federal judge, after a husband and wife had been separated for twelve months.[11] Heck saw no trouble in this respect. Belle had been gone almost that long and Judge Parker was a great admirer of Heck's. When well enough to return to his duties, Heck

Tulsa about 1890. Heck Thomas rode here often to visit Matie Mowbray. Courtesy Western History Collections, University of Oklahoma Library.

Matie Mowbray, Tulsa's second mission schoolteacher, fell in love with Heck Thomas on first sight and later married him. Courtesy Thomas Collection.

already had his mind made up. He told Matie, "Someday, I'm coming back after you."¹²

During the next three years, Heck corresponded regularly with Matie. In 1889, he transferred to the Northern District of the Federal Court which was headquartered in Vinita. He rode to Tulsa to see Matie as often as he could. Her parents liked him quite well, for like Matie, Heck was a good conversationalist. Matie knew her father thought Heck was coming to visit with him instead of her.

Reverend Mowbray was very strict. About all Heck and Matie were permitted to do together on Sunday was stroll down to the river. Or they could walk out to the cemetery and read the inscriptions on the graves. They weren't allowed to read a newspaper, book, nor do much else on Sunday.

Still Matie was hesitant about forming a permanent relationship with Heck. Previously, she had a love affair with a young man named Owen Bland. He had gone to Kansas, and she hadn't heard from him since. This troubled her considerably, but her father discouraged her in waiting for him.

In October 1891, Heck and Matie decided to get married. The only place to get a marriage license in Indian Territory was at Muskogee or Vinita, and Reverend Mowbray was the sole person in his district empowered to secure these forms. For some time, he did a large business in performing marriages.¹³ But Heck, forty-one, and Matie, eighteen, did not want to approach Reverend Mowbray about marrying them. First, they knew he would not approve of their marriage because of Heck being a divorced man and, second, because of the great difference between their ages. Instead, they eloped to Arkansas City, Kansas. Matie wrote to her mother afterwards, telling her of their wedding. Reverend Mowbray never held much regard for Heck after that.

For a time, the new Mr. and Mrs. Heck Thomas lived in a boarding house in Arkansas City. Matie found out in a hurry what it was like to be the wife of a U.S. deputy marshal. As she would for the next twenty-four years, she spent long hours at home, wondering if Heck would return. She laid around and read a lot. When Heck came home, he brought her candy. Right off, Matie began to put on weight, a problem which was to plague her the rest of her life.

Heck liked for Matie to dress well. Before, most of her clothing had come from mission barrels sent from the East. Now, Heck was making good money with all his fees and rewards, and he encouraged her to buy a number of new dresses. Some of them she kept for years, even though she could no longer get into them.

Matie was very proud of Heck and the fact that he was her husband. He was equally proud of her. His one regret was that he could not spend more time with her. But he was first and foremost a deputy marshal and things were stirring all over Indian Territory.

Chapter 7

Pursuing Ned Christie

Ned Christie, born in 1852, was a Cherokee legislator from the Going Snake District of the Cherokee Nation. He served as a member of the Executive Council for Principal Chief Dennis Bushyhead.[1] Like many young Indians, Christie had a fondness for illegal liquor and sometimes drank too much. On May 4, 1887, following a drinking party on Spring Branch in Tahlequah, Christie and several others were accused of killing Deputy Marshal Dan Maples.[2] Christie said he didn't do it, but circumstantial evidence involving him was found near the scene of the crime. The U.S. marshal issued a writ for his arrest. Fearing he could not obtain a fair trial in the white man's court, Christie refused to surrender, and went on the outlaw trail.

Soon Christie became known as one of the most vicious outlaws in the territory. Rightly or wrongly, every crime in the area was blamed on him.

In May 1887, Benjamin Harrison became president and appointed Jacob Yoes as U.S. marshal, supplanting Marshal Carroll. A husky man with a blunt looking face and dark hair, Yoes was a man of strong will and temperament.

In one of his first actions, Marshal Yoes set about cleaning up the backlog of business in the marshal's office.[3] Of

Ned Christie became known as one of the most vicious outlaws in Indian Territory. Courtesy Northeastern State University.

particular concern to him was the long pending case regarding the murder of Deputy Marshal Dan Maples. Yoes considered it unthinkable that such should go unpunished, but the case could not go to trial until Christie was arrested.

Few of the deputy marshals were anxious to go up against Christie. Holed up in his fortified home in the Rabbit Trap community with several young confederates and a deadly shot, Christie was able to fight off every deputy marshal who sought to bring him in. But Yoes was determined he must be arrested.

In August 1887, he summoned his most able deputy, Heck Thomas, who had just brought in a wagonload of prisoners. Handing him a writ for Christie, Yoes reminded Heck there was a standing reward of five hundred dollars for the Cherokee outlaw which would make his arrest worthwhile. In addition, he gave him another handful of writs and subpoenas to make his trip to Indian Territory even more profitable.

As a rule, Heck liked to man hunt alone, or with just one or two trusted posse men. This time he chose L.P. Isbell of Vinita. Isbell was a levelheaded, cautious man, a skilled tracker almost as good with a gun as Heck.

The two deputies started on the usual circuit through Indian Territory, handing out subpoenas and making arrests. By the time they reached Muskogee, they had thirteen prisoners. Leaving them under guard at Evans Stable, they met Bub Trainor, one of Tahlequah's young "Saturday night outlaws," who knew Ned Christie and the Going Snake District well.[4] The three men set out on Christie's trail. After three weeks of tracking the wily outlaw, the officers located him at his home in Rabbit Trap. Heck sought the assistance of U.S. Deputy Marshals Rusk and Salmon.[5] The five lawmen arrived in the vicinity of Christie's home before dawn on Thursday, September 26.

Heck planned to surround the house quietly, then wait for Christie to come out. But as dawn broke, the dogs in the yard began barking. Heck could hear someone "crawling to the loft."[6] He made a quick change in plans and signaled for the deputies to rush the log cabin.

Heck shouted, "United States Marshals!" He demanded that Christie surrender.[7]

Christie did not answer. Instead, he knocked a plank off the gabled end of the cabin, "gobbled" at the deputies, and opened fire. The deputies shot back. Heck warned Christie if he was going to fight to send out his women and children, that the deputies were going to set his house on fire.[8]

Christie cracked down on the lawmen with his loud Winchester. Heck "then fired a small out-building near the house," hoping to smoke him out, and all the deputies took positions behind trees "to await developments." A woman ran out of the house. The officers held their fire until she had escaped in the direction of the spring.

The shooting began again. Heck and Isbell took shelter behind the same tree. In turning around, Isbell exposed his left shoulder and Christie found his target, shattering Isbell's shoulder with his Winchester.

The flames from the outbuilding now took hold of the cabin. Smoke billowed from under the eaves. Heck waited for Christie to come out. In the early morning light, he saw a figure dash forth from the burning building and try to climb over the fence. Thinking it was Christie, Heck shouted for him to "hold up." But the figure did not, and the deputies fired, striking him three times. He fell, but managed to escape in the tall weeds.

By now, Isbell was "becoming very faint and sick." Believing Christie had escaped and fearing the woman might bring reinforcements, Heck ordered the deputies to retire to where they had left their horses.[9] The deputies rode toward Tahlequah. They were "seven hours on the road, Isbell being too sick to move rapidly."

Their arrival in town caused considerable excitement. Heck "installed Isbell in the Hotel Deflouarney," where physicians tended to his wound, and telegraphed Marshal Yoes of their ill-fated attempt to arrest Christie. After that, he returned to Rabbit Trap with his posse.

Heck scoured the community, seeking information about Christie as to whether he was dead or alive. He learned that the one who had escaped from the burning cabin and been shot during their gun battle had been Christie's twelve-year-old son. Christie had been shot in the forehead and the boy left him unconscious in the blazing building. However, Christie had been rescued by other relatives and friends who lived nearby, and was now being hid in the hills. The deputies found the wounded boy, but there was considerable animosity toward them in the neighborhood because of the incident, and they could learn little more about Christie.

Returning to Tahlequah, Heck found Isbell improved, but after several days, seeing he could do nothing for him, he and his posse gathered his prisoners at Muskogee and returned to Fort Smith. There Heck reported to Marshal Yoes that Christie was up and around, "not withstanding his wound in the forehead," and the boy who was shot was recovering.[10]

Christie's handsome face had been disfigured and he lost the sight in his left eye. His son had been wounded and his home destroyed, all for a crime he said he didn't commit. He now swore he would never surrender nor be taken alive. Feeling secure in a rock fort built upon a hill near his burned home and surrounded by friends, he sent word to Deputy

Marshal Heck Thomas where he could be found and informed him that if he thought he could capture him to come and they would shoot it out.

Challenged by Christie's message, after spending a month in Fort Smith settling his accounts and testifying in various court cases, Heck began organizing his posse for the return trip to Rabbit Trap. He left Fort Smith on November 6, taking with him Deputies Bub Trainor, James Farr, and Britt Simmons. Along the way, they picked up Joe Caudel, Sam Simmons, John McEachin, and James McNolly.[11]

The posse reached Rabbit Trap on November 12. Heck found Christie entrenched in his fort on the mountaintop, daring them to approach. Heck discussed the situation with the other deputies. Most of them believed "it would take a large regiment of U.S. militia to stand up to Christie and the powerful defense surrounding him."[12] Heck decided he did not want to expose his men needlessly to the danger. He called off the assault and contented himself with scouring the neighborhood for information about Christie and the boy before leaving the community with his posse.[13]

This was Heck's final attempt to capture Christie. He had succeeded in filling the Cherokee outlaw with a burning hatred for all white men. It would be another three years before Marshal Yoes' deputies would succeed in blasting Christie out of his new fortified home and killing him. Meantime, circumstances decreed to Heck that it was time for him to be moving on.

Chapter 8

Chasing Outlaws in Oklahoma Territory

Following the Civil War, the Federal government took the western half of Indian Territory from the Five Civilized Tribes to settle other tribes upon the land. When all was done, about two million acres remained in the heart of Oklahoma Territory unassigned to any tribe.

The Oklahoma Boomers, led first by Kansan David Payne and then William Couch, finally succeeded in getting the government to open the Unassigned Lands to settlement. On April 22, 1889, more than one hundred thousand settlers gathered on the borders of the land to stake their claims in a land rush. By nightfall, tent cities had sprung up all over the area, and thousands of people milled about.

Congress, in its haste to open the Unassigned Lands had failed to establish any type of local government for the territory. Only a handful of U.S. deputy marshals and soldiers were available to maintain law and order. A new Western District of the Federal Court was established at Guthrie, the capital of Oklahoma Territory. For some time, Heck Thomas had been unhappy working in the Fort Smith court under Marshal Jacob Yoes, whom he considered a very strict man and hard to get along with. Therefore, he applied for a

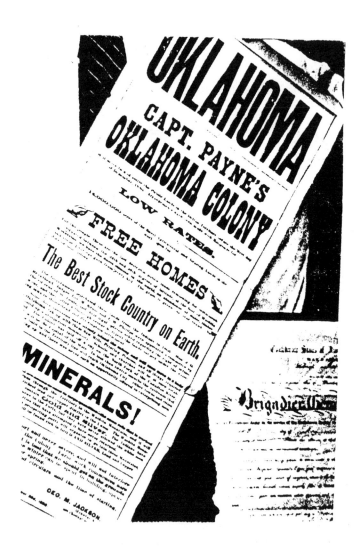

Handbills boosting settlement of the Unassigned Lands found their way across the country and encouraged many a settler to congregate on the border in hopes of obtaining free land. Courtesy Norman Transcript.

deputy's commission in Oklahoma Territory and transferred to Guthrie.

At Guthrie, Heck met two men with whom he was to for a lifelong friendship. They were U.S. Deputy Marshals Chris Madsen and William "Bill" Tilghman. Together the three of them would rack up such a record of law enforcement they would gain fame as "The Three Guardsmen" for their valor in bringing law and order to Oklahoma Territory.

Of medium height with a pleasant face and a well-trained, dark mustache, Bill Tilghman had already established a name for himself before coming to Guthrie. He had been city marshal at Dodge City, Kansas, during its rowdy days as a shipping point for Texas trail herds, and for two years served as deputy sheriff of Ford County, Kansas, under Bat Masterson. Quiet and courteous, Tilghman was well known for his feats with a gun, though he always said he preferred peaceable arrests to gun slinging.[1]

Chris Madsen was a short, portly man with merry, blue eyes and a thick accent, who hailed from Denmark. A professional soldier, he had fought in the Danish army when fourteen-years-old, then spent five years in the French Foreign Legion.[2] After that, he came to the United States and joined the army. He was assigned to Custer's 7th Cavalry, but fortunately was transferred to the 5th Cavalry before Custer's fateful trek to the Little Bighorn. Madsen had served fifteen years in the army before joining the U.S. marshal's service.

The Three Guardsmen soon proved to be an unbeatable combination. Each was an expert shot and of high moral character. Though Heck still preferred riding alone on his man hunting quests or with a favored few men, when the situation demanded, he didn't hesitate to team up with Tilghman and Madsen and their posses.

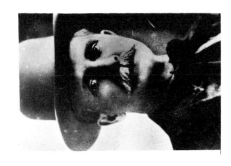

"The Three Guardsmen," from left, U.S. Deputy Marshals Bill Tilghman, **Heck Thomas**, and Chris Madsen remained lifelong friends. Courtesy **Thomas Collection**.

There was plenty of activity in the new territory to keep all of the deputies busy. Following the opening of the Unassigned Lands, others land openings followed. Along with the honest, hardworking settlers came the riffraff. Hordes of outlaws and crooks poured into the region with no other purpose than to rob, to cheat, or to hide from the law. Among them flourished some of the worst outlaw gangs in American history, including those of the Daltons and Bill Doolin.

The Dalton brothers, Emmett, Grat, Frank, and Bob had once served as deputy marshals out of Fort Smith. Bill Dalton had been a California legislator. In 1885, Frank was killed in a gun battle with bootleggers in the river bottoms west of Fort Smith.[3] Heck had tracked down Frank's slayer soon after and won the gratitude of all the Dalton family.

It came as a surprise to everyone then, in 1890, to learn that Emmett, Bob, and Grat had been involved in horse stealing.[4] The three men fled to California where they robbed a Southern Pacific train on February 6, 1891, fatally wounding the fireman. Authorities posted a five thousand dollar reward for the Daltons. Bob and Emmett sped back toOklahoma Territory. Grat had been captured, but soon he escaped and rejoined his brothers. The trio collected a gang and settled down to serious outlaw business.[5]

In short order, the Dalton gang robbed the Santa Fe passenger train at Wharton, the Katy north of Wagoner, the Santa Fe at Red Rock, and the Katy at Adair Station in the Cherokee Nation, and a bank in El Reno. Several passengers and lawmen had been killed during the course of these robberies. The reward for the Daltons jumped to forty thousand dollars for apprehension and conviction. With this stipulation, most man hunters considered the amount of the reward not worth the risk of tackling the dangerous gang.[6]

But Heck, now married to Matie and living in Guthrie, made up his mind to get the Daltons. He hoped to find them and talk them into giving themselves up. He believed there was not sufficient evidence to convict the brothers.[7]

Heck joined with Fred Dodge, Chief Detective for the Wells Fargo Express Co., for the expedition. The express company outfitted them with two horses and special saddlebags.[8] Taking Burrell Cox, a former deputy under Grat Dalton, the three lawmen disappeared into the Creek Nation. All firmly believed they would return with the gang in tow.

The lawmen spent six weeks trailing the Daltons. They obtained "full information" about their movements and were about ready to lead a posse to take them when the gang suddenly pulled out, and Heck and Dodge lost track of them.[9]

The Daltons were not long in resurfacing. In Coffeyville, Kansas, on October 5, 1892, they attempted to rob two banks at once. In the shootout which resulted, four members of the gang, including Grat and Bob Dalton, and four citizens were killed. Emmett Dalton was severely wounded and captured.

As soon as Heck and Detective Dodge received news of the shootings, they went to Coffeyville to make "proof of death" of the Daltons for Wells Fargo. Emmett Dalton served fourteen years in prison. In later years, he confided to Heck that he had been the "nemesis" of the gang, trying to bait them into traps during his six-week chase. Though the gang did not spring the traps, Emmett said Heck had made it too hot for them.[10] With law and order coming to the territory, they knew they could not stay here much longer. After pulling this last big raid at Coffeyville, they had planned on going to South America.[11]

Wells Fargo Express Co. also felt Heck's efforts, more than anything else, had brought about the extermination of the

Dalton gang. In appreciation, Manager Andrews sent him a check for fifteen hundred dollars.[12]

Grover Cleveland had won a second term as President, and when he took office again in March 1893, he made a clean sweep of the Republican appointees and placed new men in office as was the general rule. Heck applied for the marshal's position at Guthrie. Several leaders of the Democratic Central Committee and county officers wrote, endorsing him for the job. But Heck failed to get the position. Instead, the political plum went to Evett Dumas Nix, a Guthrie businessman with no experience in law enforcement.

Early that year, the government announced that the Cherokee Outlet, a narrow strip of land in Oklahoma Territory adjoining the southern border of Kansas, would be opened for settlement in September. Marshal Nix immediately called for one hundred and fifty deputies to quell the disorder expected in the opening. To those who applied, he stated his requirements were that all of his staff must be above reproach and not drink.[13] Among the first deputies he commissioned were Heck Thomas, Chris Madsen, and Bill Tilghman.

When his staff was completed, Nix called his deputies together for a three-day conference.[14] He laid down ironclad rules for the personal conduct of his men, and urged them to never forget they were facing the wildest characters on the frontier. (This from a greenhorn talking to well-experienced men such as The Three Guardsmen!) Nix ordered his men to safeguard their own lives and that of others by always getting the drop on the other fellow before they commanded him to hold up his hands. No doubt Heck Thomas walked away from this conference shaking his head.

For a time, the news that one hundred and fifty deputies were patrolling the Cherokee Outlet kept the outlaws quiet.

Heck had not forgotten, though, that Bill Doolin, a member of the Dalton gang, had escaped the fight at Coffeyville. A slow, deliberate fellow, on the way to Coffeyville Doolin had told the others in the gang that his horse had gone lame so he dropped out of the raid. Afterwards, some wondered how much truth there was in his story.[15] For it was rumored that Doolin had got into an argument with Bob Dalton, the impulsive, twenty-two-year-old leader of the Kansas raid, saying the double robbery was too daring and dangerous. If so, subsequent events bore out the truth of Doolin's words.

Following his narrow escape from the gunfight at Coffeyville, Doolin immediately gathered a new gang. Among the members was Bill Dalton who had hurried to Oklahoma Territory from California on hearing of the deaths of his brothers. Dalton burned for revenge against the law officers. In quick succession, the Doolin gang struck at banks in Spearville, Kansas; Southwest City, Missouri; Bentonville, Arkansas; and Caney, Kansas. They robbed trains near Canadian, Texas, Red Rock, Pryor, and Dover Creek in Indian Territory.

At the height of their activity in the Territory, the Bill Doolin gang became so notorious that Judge Frank Dale, in charge of the Federal Court in Guthrie, told the U.S. deputy marshals to quit trying to bring the gang in alive. Chris Madsen asked if he really meant that, to which Judge Dale replied that he did.[16]

Much of the time, the Doolin gang hid out near Ingalls, a small, out-of-the-way place in the Cherokee Outlet. When in town, they were treated almost royally because they brought money into the town.

The marshal's office in Guthrie soon learned the whereabouts of the Doolin gang. Bill Tilghman planned to lead a raid to capture them. Then he broke his leg and couldn't go.[17] Nor did Heck go. He said afterwards that he had been asked to join the deputies but, "I didn't like their plans, and the result was as I predicted."[18]

In the gun battle with the Doolin gang, which ensued in Ingalls on September 1, 1893, three deputies and three citizens were killed, and Bill Doolin escaped again. The remainder of the gang went into hiding for awhile.

Two weeks later on September 16, the Cherokee Outlet opened to settlement in one of the biggest land rushes yet. More than one hundred thousand people poured into the area. Things at Perry (formerly Wharton) became so violent within a week, Marshal Nix sent Heck and Tilghman there to assist. Heck was in charge of guarding the land office.

The first thing the new mayor did on taking office was to appoint Tilghman as city marshal and Heck as his assistant. Marshal Nix gave them leave to accept the jobs while retaining their deputy commissions.

Meeting each situation as circumstances warranted, Heck and Tilghman soon pushed out the vicious element. They reduced the number of saloons in town from 110 to 52. Those that remained were told they would have to purchase a yearly license at three hundred dollars.

This produced opposition within the city council. For it was an axiom on the border that where saloons and gambling houses flourished the town could do likewise. Councilman Gregg insisted that Perry would die if not allowed to run wide open.[19] He believed that Heck was the one behind the closing of so many saloons. At a council meeting in February 1894, he demanded Heck's resignation and verbally assaulted him. Heck replied in kind, and Gregg threw an inkwell at him, which missed.

At the next city council meeting, on the night of February 24, 1894, another councilman, Lauren Drake, physically assailed Heck.[20] The lawman pounded him over the head with a billy club. The council fired Heck and a policeman called "Fatty," in a special meeting. But Heck remained on the payroll until April when a Republican mayor took over and named a new police force.

By then, Perry was settling down, and Heck was anxious to get back to Guthrie. He and Matie had moved there early in 1893. She had gone with him to Perry, too, but they both liked Guthrie better. They purchased a small house in Guthrie at 909 East Springer, which is still standing.

It was here in July 1895, that their first child, Henry Lovick Thomas, was born. Matie absolutely adored "Baby Heck," as she always called him.

On July 15, 1895, according to a note in one of Heck's day books, he made a trip to Georgia to see his other family. When he returned, he brought Albert back with him. Now fifteen-years-old, Albert had always loved his father and wanted to be like him. He lived with Heck and Matie and began riding for Heck. Sometimes it was difficult for Matie to get along with her stepson, for he was not much younger than she.

Albert was very handsome. He spoke good English and made a fine appearance. But on one score, he was a big disappointment to his father. "He was a great lover of poetry," Albert recalled once, "and was disappointed in me that I did not care for it at all. I have many times heard him recite certain things from Scott, Byron, and others."[21]

Albert was not the only one of Heck's family now living in the Territory. His uncle, Gen. Edward Thomas, under whom he had served as courier during the Civil War, had received appointment to a position in the U.S. Land Department in

1885. In June 1893, he became the agent of the Fox-Sac Agency in Indian Territory. Uncle Ed was of medium height, "well-knit" and proportioned. He had white hair, a kindly face and puffed continuously on a pipe, recalling wartime anecdotes to all who would listen. He maintained a fine, gracious home near the agency, reminiscent of those in the old South.[22] Heck's eldest daughter, Belle Fullwood Thomas, worked for Uncle Ed at the agency for a time. Heck visited them there, and Uncle Ed came to Guthrie on at least one occasion shortly after Albert's arrival.[23]

For a time, Heck was content with his family and friends around him, doing the type of work he loved best. But there was still much lawlessness and whiskey peddling going on in the Territory, and Bill Doolin had resurfaced.

Chapter 9

The Bill Doolin Gang

Following the disastrous raid on the Dalton gang in Ingalls on September 1, 1893, Bill Doolin had gone into hiding in New Mexico. He took with him his wife, Edith Ellsworth, the daughter of a Methodist preacher whom he had married in the spring of that year. Now he was back.

Afraid that Doolin would reorganize his gang and start terrorizing the Twin Territories again, Deputy Marshal Bill Tilghman spent weeks trailing him. Finally, he tracked him down on a farm near Burden, Kansas, where the outlaw and his family lived so poorly in a tent by the river, that the church wives of Burden had brought them a gift of supplies at Christmas.[1] But by the time Tilghman arrived, he found Edith and their two-year-old child had gone to visit her father who lived near Lawson (now Quay, Oklahoma). Plagued by rheumatism, Doolin had traveled to Eureka Springs, Arkansas, to ease his ailment in the hot springs.

Unwilling to give up the chase, Tilghman followed Doolin and arrested "the king of the outlaws" in Eureka Springs on January 15, 1896, singlehandedly and without firing a shot.[2] On the outlaw's word of honor that he would not try to escape, he brought Doolin back to Guthrie on the train, without handcuffs.

Heck met them at the depot with a coach. A crowd had gathered to see the noted desperado. Doolin looked peaceable enough.

One small woman edged up to him and said, "Why, Mr. Doolin, you don't look so bad. I believe I could capture you myself."[3]

To which Doolin looked down at her and spoke with a grin: "Yes, ma'm, I believe you could."

The deputies locked Doolin in the federal jail, across the street from the Guthrie depot. During the next few months, the famed outlaw acted as a model prisoner. But Heck warned the other deputies that Doolin was still a dangerous man and should be watched closely. His words proved prophetic. On the evening of July 5, Doolin escaped with thirteen other prisoners in a major jailbreak. Heck had walked up town to mail some letters. As soon as he heard the news, he ran home to get his Winchester.[4]

Excitedly, he warned Matie, "Those men who escaped from the jail will want guns. They will know that I have fine weapons and may know where I live. I want you to hide my guns."

As soon as Heck left, Matie obediently took his extra rifles and six-shooters and hid them in the tall grass and brush behind the house. The next evening when Heck returned from a fruitless search, "he was terribly put out," Matie related to her daughter, Beth, years later, to find that his "precious" guns had been left out in the weather.

"Why, woman," Heck scolded Matie, "those guns will rust—I wouldn't have them rusted for anything."He spent hours polishing and rubbing those guns.

"—And after I had helped by hiding them!" Matie said in chagrin.

After gathering supplies for a concentrated search, Heck set off on Doolin's trail again. For nearly a month he followed him. Heck always operated on the theory that all one had to do to find a bad man was to locate his wife or sweetheart. Afterwards, Edith Doolin thought it was John Matthews, a half-breed Indian who had married her sister, who had tipped off the officers as to Doolin's whereabouts. But it was a neighbor, Bee Dunn, who said that Edith was at her father's house near Lawson.[5] Heck rode there at once to put the place under surveillance.

As expected, Doolin soon showed up. Heck rounded up a nine-man posse, including his son, Albert, John Matthews, Tom Noble, Charles Noble, and the Dunn brothers.

The Ellsworth farmhouse sat on a high hill. When the posse arrived and the men placed themselves in hiding around the house, it was dark and Doolin had a wagon backed up to the porch, loading furniture. He planned to return New Mexico and start a new life with his family. But, unfortunately for him, it was too late.

Many stories have been told about what happened next. Perhaps the most accurate account is that written by Heck in a letter to Tilghman a few days later:[6]

> Guthrie, Okla.
> Sept. 3, 1896
>
> Dear Bill-
>
> The day before I got last news of Doolin, I was 14 miles beyond Chandler, and drove through in one day. Next day I got a telegraph message that Doolin and four others were in the Ingalls country and I started for Bo Dunn's—had Rufus Cannon and Albert with me. Made the drive by 2 o'clock and, after getting to Dunn's, got

the news that carried me beyond Lawson. Met the Noble boys and some others with fresh news, and made a run of about four miles on "Limber Jim"—got to where two of the gang had been that night, and crawled up close enough to watch old Ellsworth's house with Bill Cook's field glasses.

We waited a long time without seeing anyone, although there was considerable stir about the store and dugout. Finally he came out of the stable and, to our great surprise, started down the lane, coming west. You know how the store is situated on high prairie. If he had wanted to have made his escape, he could have had open roads north, south, east, northeast, southeast, or northwest through the pasture to those high hills that you have seen many times.

He came straight down the lane leading his horse by the bridle reins, walking in the bright moonlight, Winchester in both hands, well out in front of him, nearly in a position to shoot. He was walking slow, looking first on one side and then on the other. He was sure on the prod, and was looking for the neighborhood boys that had been spying on him, intending to shoot them up a little. When I hollered to him and had one of the boys on the other side of the road holler to him, right after I did, he shot at me and the bullet passed between me and Bee Dunn. I had let one of the boys have my Winchester, and had the old Number 8 shotgun. It was too long in the breach and I couldn't handle it quick, so he got in another shot with his Winchester, and, as he dropped his Winchester from a glancing shot on it, he jerked out his pistol. Some of the boys thought he shot once with it and the others twice. At about that time I got the shotgun to work and the fight was over.

HECK

Edith Doolin ran screaming to the scene. Heck told her Doolin was dead and in the hands of the law, and she could not see him. He and his men loaded the body into a borrowed spring wagon. Edith followed the officers to Guthrie in another wagon. In town, the citizens went wild in celebration, relieved at the death of the noted desperado.

Heck put the wagon and mules on a vacant lot next to his house. Matie had an Irish woman named Maggie Murphy who worked for her. Maggie came running into the house.

"Oh, Mrs. Thomas! Have the men take that wagon away. The hay in it is all bloody and the mules are eating it!"

Heck took the hay out of the wagon and burned the hay and washed out the wagon.

The next day, the Wells Fargo Express Company gave Heck a reward for the capture of Bill Doolin. The following month, the State of Missouri voted to give him another five hundred dollars, and one of the railroads gave him three hundred dollars.[7] Of this amount, Heck kept only four hundred dollars. Matie asked him about the remainder of the thirteen hundred dollars.

Heck hesitated a moment, then said, "Now, Mate, the boys on the posse risked their lives, too, just as much as I did, and I—well, I just split the money with them!"[8]

He didn't even hold out his expenses. Matie did not fuss at Heck. She knew that although he didn't like to earn his pay by being forced to kill men, still he wanted to take care of the "boys" who worked with him. He split part of the money with Tilghman, too. Tilghman hadn't received a dime for all his efforts in tracking down Bill Doolin the first time, because the posted rewards had been for conviction only.[9]

When shot, Bill Doolin had twenty-one bullet holes in him. The next day at the morgue someone made the remark that it looked as if the officers had found him dead then shot him full of holes.[10] This story has resurfaced many times since then, but it wasn't true, according to Matie. She had heard the story too

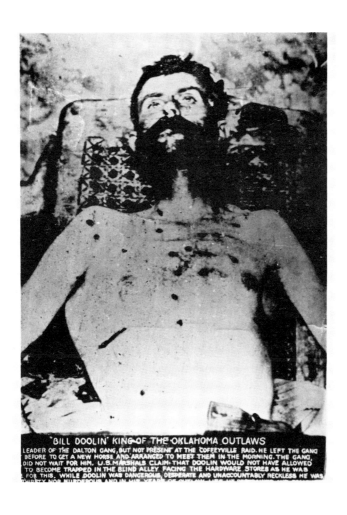

Bill Doolin, "King of the Oklahoma Outlaws," was shot and killed by Heck Thomas and his posse. Courtesy Thomas Collection.

many times from Heck and Albert to believe otherwise. She knew they did not lie.

Heck's homecoming from the capture of Doolin was not all on the bright side. While he was off man hunting, Baby Heck took sick with what Matie called *cholera fantum*. He died on August 5, 1896, at the age of thirteen months, and was buried before Heck's return.

After Doolin's death, the rest of his gang was soon captured or shot. The last of these outlaws was "Little Dick" West. For a time West hooked up with the Al Jennings gang. Al Jennings was a lawyer and the son of a former Woodward judge. Together with his brothers John and Ed, Jennings headed one of the most laughable outlaw gangs in the history of the Territory. In existence only three months, practically everything the Jennings gangs did turned out wrong. They held up several trains and robbed a bank, but about all they ever got was a stalk of bananas, a two-gallon jug of whiskey, and four hundred dollars.[11]

Disgusted with the bumbling of the Jennings gang, West left them. Heck trailed him to the border of the Creek Nation in Indian Territory. He notified U.S. Deputy Marshal Bud Ledbetter that West was in his area. West eluded Ledbetter's pursuit and headed back to Oklahoma Territory. Heck trailed him to a ranch west of Guthrie. On April 6, 1896, with Chief Deputy Bill Fossett, Sheriff Frank Rhinehart, Deputy Tilghman, and Albert, Heck gave West a chance to surrender. But the outlaw went for his guns and he died without firing a shot.[12]

With the death of Little Dick West, the era of big time outlaws in the Twin Territories ended. The raw, new country was settling down. Heck had done much to help bring this about, capturing all kinds of law breakers and bringing them to justice. He worked long, hard hours in the burning heat of summer and chilling winds of winter for more than a decade. His bed was nearly always on the ground with his saddle for a pillow. Many times during the winter, he awoke to find himself covered with snow. Often he ate skimpy meals of bread and meat washed down with water. Now forty-six, rheumatism racked his body.[13]

Despite all the hardships that he endured and the constant threat of death, Heck never lost sight of the fact that he was the legal representative of the law in the turbulent territories—and that he, therefore, had to live and act as was expected of him. He gave the murderers that he faced the opportunity to surrender, and thus live; if they resisted, he shot to kill. Few men dared draw against him, for his reputation as a lighting-fast gun-thrower, possessed of a deadly skill, cowed them.[14]

With the country settling down, life in general seemed to do so for the Thomas family. On February 15, 1897, six months after the death of Baby Heck, Matie gave birth to a daughter, Harley. This eased the pain of her loss of Baby Heck somewhat, though the rest of her life she could never bring herself to talk about him without tears in her eyes.

The following spring, Uncle Ed died in South McAlester on March 8, 1898. He was buried in Oak Hill Cemetery at Kiowa in Pittsburg County, Indian Territory. His marker designated him as Colonel Thomas instead of General Thomas. Presumably his promotion to general had been a brevet command, good only for the duration of the war.

A few days after Uncle Ed died, Albert married. Four weeks later, leaving his bride, he marched off to the Spanish American War to storm San Juan Hill with Teddy Roosevelt's troopers.[15]

Heck and Matie's third and youngest child, Beth, was born on June 21, 1899, in the little house in Guthrie. Much to Matie's regret, Heck was out man hunting that night, too.

Heck continued as a U.S. deputy marshal in the Guthrie district for two more years. Then on August 6, 1901, the Kiowa-Comanche reservation in the southern part of Oklahoma Territory opened for settlement. Heck turned in that direction and soon began a whole new phase of his law keeping career.

Chapter 10

City Marshal of Lawton

Early in the spring of 1901, President McKinley announced he was going to open the Comanche lands in southern Oklahoma Territory to settlement. This time, to prevent the abuses and excesses which had existed in the previous land openings in Oklahoma Territory and the Cherokee Outlet, government officials elected to settle the Comanche lands by lottery instead of a run.[1]

Heck Thomas had been interested in that area for several years. He held a commission in that district under United States Marshal Thompson at Anadarko. He had made his first trip into the Comanche country in 1886 when he captured a Negro at Fort Sill, who was wanted in Texas for assault upon a white girl. At that time, Heck discussed the possibilities of the land with W. H. Quinette, the trader at the fort, who still operated the post office there.[2]

Since then, Heck had ventured into the Comanche country many times on official business. He liked the wide-open spaces with the nearby mountains. This would be a good place to settle down if a man got a chance, he thought. But for now, he had other things to think about.

In May, the government began surveying the Comanche lands, and established three town sites within them. One was

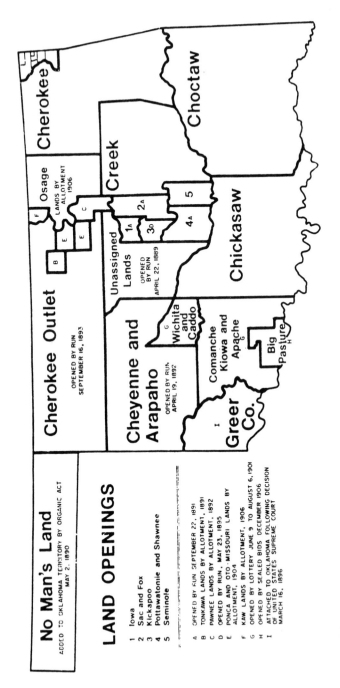

Oklahoma Land Openings.

located at present Lawton on the eastern side of the Wichita Mountains, one at Hobart on the western side, and the third at Anadarko to the north. Registration points for the lottery were set up at Fort Sill and at Fort El Reno. Registration was scheduled to begin on July 10, 1901, and to close on July 26.

Before the lottery, United States Marshal William D. Fossett assigned Heck Thomas and five other deputy marshals to patrol the Lawton townsite.

By the first of July, the crowds began to move in. Fort Sill then was a mere outpost with a scattering of buildings and dirty, flapping tents. The Lawton town site could be reached only by dirt road. The nearest railroad to Fort Sill was at Marlow and Rush Springs on the eastern edge of the Comanche reservation. Therefore, three-fourths of the settlers went to El Reno to register.[3]

They came by every mode of transportation, wagons so old drivers had to stop every few miles to drive an iron wheel back on; in buggies so new they glistened. Women and children plodded behind milk cows. Men walked with packs on their backs. Some rode spirited horses. All were making the trek to the last frontier.

The actual drawing for the 320-acre homesteads was slated for September 30 at El Reno.[4] Beginning August 6, lots in the three town sites would be sold. While awaiting the results of the drawing and sale of the town sites, thousands of the hopeful established temporary homes, offices, and business places in tents near the town sites. Actually, there was little to draw them to the new lands. Neither the climate with its extremes in weather, nor the flat, featureless plains seemed enticing. Only one tree existed on the Lawton town site, but intoxicated by the thought of free land, the purchase of a valuable town lot, or just a new beginning, the settlers came and dreamed.

Following the land lottery at El Reno on September 30, thousands more disappointed land seekers descended upon the three town sites, hoping to buy a lot cheap.

By August 5, an estimated twenty thousand people were camped on the east and south sides of Lawton's mile-square town site. Two major thoroughfares formed between the tents, one that everyone called "Main Street" and the other "Goo Goo Avenue."[5]

The whole area presented a "Klondike scene."[6] Thousands of tents jutted out of the plains like mushrooms, mules and horses kicked up dust. Smoke rose from campfires, women and children sat listlessly on boxes, and the hot sun blazed down on everything.

Neither ice, shade, nor sanitary conveniences were to be had. Water sold for twenty-five cents a bucket. Dust blew over everything, and the incessant flap of the tents in the wind wore everyone's nerves to a frazzle. Dogs barked, mules brayed, men called, and the fakirs harangued. To add to the confusion, one thousand Comanches pitched their tents nearby.[7]

The main attraction in the tent city was "Goo Goo" Avenue. This street was named for a young woman who had come to Lawton with a traveling tent show. Known as "The Flying Lady," each night Miss Shaffer could be heard all along that section of town singing: "Just because you made those goo goo eyes at me . . . ."

On Goo Goo Avenue, the tents were packed "so close tent ropes seemed wound around each other."[8] The terms of the town site sale dictated the buyer must have cash. This attracted the rougher elements to the area. Robberies and pickpocketing occurred daily. Gambling tents with all sorts of gambling devices ran day and night. The taking of life seemed so common in Lawton it created no excitement, according to the local newspapers.[9]

The crowds far outnumbered what Fossett and his deputies had expected. They could not cope with the disorder. They were further handicapped in that they could not arrest anyone unless they violated a federal law. Thus, the tent city quickly became a gambler's paradise.[10]

"Fifty assistants would have been little enough considering the fact that we are all trespassers alike and the outlaws soon understood this condition," grumbled the unhappy editor of the Lawton *Daily Democrat*. "Saloons and their general results will be added to the present deplorable state."[11]

Spread too few and working day and night, Fossett and his deputies began to feel desperate over their inability to control the corruption on Goo Goo Avenue. Then two days before the opening of the town site, the officers received an unexpected assist from the responsible citizens of the new town when they decided to put Goo Goo Avenue out of business.

The whole thing began that Sunday morning at ten o'clock when an old soldier was robbed of his pension in a shell game.[12] A sympathetic crowd quickly gathered and raided the gambling tent. They cut the tent ropes, and it collapsed. They captured the gambler, intending to hang him. Fossett and his deputies, rode up on horseback and rescued the gambler. At this, the mob grew angrier.

The citizens followed the deputies to the courthouse square, where the deputies had a tent set up as an office. The deputies placed the gambler inside the tent, then formed a protective semicircle outside.

With the other deputies beside him, Marshal Fossett drew a line before the crowd. "Anyone who crosses that line will be shot," he warned the menacing men.

The crowd had grown bigger as it approached the square. A tall, light-complexioned man with a barrel-chest led the way.[13] When within one hundred feet of the tent, the mob began to falter. Forty feet more and it stopped.

The leader glanced back. "I'm from Texas. Follow me, men, and we'll clean them up!" he shouted.

But the mob refused to go any farther.

Fossett rode forward. "Do you want to see people killed here for a few dollars?"

"What does a life amount to?" the Texan responded. He snapped his fingers. "It doesn't amount to that!"

Nevertheless, after a moment, he turned back to the crowd. "Let's go back and clean out those gamblers."

Within thirty minutes, all the gambling houses along Goo Goo Avenue had been destroyed.[14] This effectively put a damper on gambling activities in the new town. Heck and the other deputies knew this action warned the riffraff that the responsible citizens of Lawton intended to have law and order.

By now, the crowd at Lawton was estimated at forty thousand people. On Tuesday morning, August 6, it pressed around the government auction station, which had been erected before the land office, the only wooden building on the town site. When the sale of the lots began at nine a.m., the deputies watched as it proceeded in orderly fashion.

The purchase of a lot required a twenty-five-dollar deposit. The buyer had thirty minutes to obtain the balance of the money. Those who didn't have time to secure their funds from where they had secreted them, or from the temporary wooden bank placed on wheels outside the town site, lost their deposit and the lot was resold at once. As soon as a sale was made, federal soldiers conducted the buyer between two lines to the land office. There the sale was concluded. The new owner had the privilege of immediately moving onto his lot and begin building.

Sheriff W.W. Painter had set a covered wagon on the southwest corner of the square for a temporary courthouse. When the sale of lots began, county officers, who had been appointed, began taking their oaths of office there. Sheriff Painter chained his first prisoners to the wagon. One of them escaped, taking the wheel with him. Deputies found the prisoner later along Cache Creek still carrying the wheel.[15]

By August 8, the best lots in Lawton had been sold. All that summer and fall of 1901, one could scarcely sleep day or night for the constant beat of the hammer and rasp of the saw as the building of homes and businesses continued. On top of this sounded the continual "tum-tum-tum" of the Comanche drums.

"The noise was so great," said one, "even the well wished to die."[16]

Dust storms and lack of water added to the difficulties. Still, it seemed to Heck that the town rose as if by magic. On September 24, the first Chicago, Rock Island & Pacific train steamed into town. Lots which had sold for fifty dollars each a few weeks before now changed hands at three hundred dollars and up. Heck decided that Lawton had a great future ahead of it. Having always liked this part of the Territory, he decided he might like to become part of it.

That chance came sooner than he expected. On September 6, Lawton, as elsewhere, was stunned by the news of the attempted assassination of President McKinley. He died eight days later, and Theodore Roosevelt took over as president.

Heck expected that Roosevelt, as was the custom, would make a clean sweep of previous appointees and put men of his own political persuasion in office. Heck had never failed to

Lawton shortly after the land opening. Courtesy Western History Collections, University of Oklahoma Library.

obtain a commission from whichever political party was in power. But he knew he was a strong Democrat and Roosevelt was an equally strong Republican. Too, he recognized that he was growing older and worn out from his long years of service in the field.

In September, when the machinery for the first Lawton city election was put into effect, Lesley P. Ross, a candidate for mayor, approached Heck about running for city marshal. Lawton needed someone like him to bring order out of the chaos, he said. Heck didn't take much time thinking over his proposition. With a steady job in one place, he could move his family to Lawton. His old friends were moving on. Bill Tilghman had taken a claim during the opening of the Fox and Sac lands and now operated a prosperous ranch in Lincoln County. Chris Madsen had returned to Federal service in the Western District as office deputy. The days of the big bandits were over. The land was changing. It was time for Heck to change, too. He said yes.

From the viewpoint of those who knew Heck, the Democrat party couldn't have chosen a better candidate for city marshal. Courteous and kind, he was always a gentleman. He went out of his way to do a favor for others. He never acted harshly or unreasonably with the unfortunates who came under his authority. He had nerves of steel and a temperament that did not let him hesitate to draw a gun and use it if necessary. The voters evidently agreed with his friends. Heck won the election for city marshal handily by a majority of sixty-three votes. He took office on October 24, 1901.[17]

Shortly after, he sent for his family. Matie, Harley, now four-years-old, and Beth, two-years-old, arrived on the train as soon as possible. For a time, they lived in a tent on the courthouse square, next to Perry Foster, the town jailor.[18] The blind Thomas Gore, who was to become a well-known Oklahoma senator, lived there, too.

After taking office, Heck organized a four-man police force which quickly grew to fourteen which included Leka Hammon, Harry Foster, Bill Bruce, Charles Hammonds, Rufus La Fors, Perry Foster, A.S. Woody, Sam Elrod, Fred Larrance, D.R. Morton, John Heatherington, S.B. Lancaster, and H.R. Blanding as police judge.[19]

Heck chose Col. J.W. "Will" Hawkins as his assistant chief of police. Six-foot-six and a handsome man, Colonel Hawkins was a professional gambler. But he knew how to use a gun and was a native Georgian. A typical Southern gentleman like Heck, the children loved Hawkins. Every where he went, the young ones crowded around him. But Hawkins was as fearless a man as he was polite, and Heck trusted his ability implicitly. Colonel Hawkins lost no time in proving that he took his new job seriously. The citizens soon forgot about his gambling reputation in light of his genial and capable disposition.

The city ordered new blue coats with bright brass buttons for the Lawton police force. Broad-brimmed hats completed their uniform. Under the patrol of Chief Heck Thomas and his new officers, the bars and streets of Lawton became peaceful, and they stayed that way. Outlaws knew to stay away.

The first police department was located in an alley at Fourth Avenue and D Street. In the beginning, the officers took all their prisoners to Fort Sill. Eventually, workers completed a new city hall at 219 D Street, and the police department moved into the large, wooden building. The new headquarters had a primitive but effective alarm system. When the gong struck once, the message was for Heck, when struck twice it was for Hawkins. When it rang three or more times that sent everybody running.

Lawton's first police force, from l., Chief Heck Thomas, Al Goff, Henry Signor, William Gentry, and Col. Will Hawkins. **Courtesy Thomas Collection.**

One day in November, three bells sent Chief Thomas and his police force rushing into the street where they were greeted by a tremendous burst of gunfire. What they saw was a large flock of geese which had settled down in the street just at sundown. The citizens were making the most of the situation. Heck ordered the police to stop the shooting at once before someone got hurt. But not until he had shot a couple of ducks to take home, too, so noted the newspaper editor.[20]

Frank Wright, Lawton pioneer newspaper publisher, chuckled again when he recalled what he termed Heck's amazing ability to draw a gun. Frequently when they met, if no one else was around, Heck amuse Wright by drawing his .45, tipping his hat and saying, "Good morning, Frank," all at the same time.[21]

Not long after the opening of the Lawton townsite, Heck moved his family from the tent on the courthouse square into a small house at 712 C Street, which belonged to Al Jennings, the outlaw.

Following his arrest and trial for robbery, on October 25, 1899, Jennings had been sentenced to life imprisonment in the penitentiary at Columbus, Ohio. But through the efforts of his brother, John, and Judge Amos Ewing, a friend of the family at Kingfisher, President McKinley had commuted Al Jennings' life sentence to five years with time off for good conduct. When released Jennings returned to Oklahoma Territory. Like thousands of others, he had come to the opening at Lawton seeking a new start. He now lived with his brother, John, and sister-in-law, Lizzie, on Avenue H between Third and Fourth Streets while renting the house he had built to Heck, his former foe.

Thomas Gore now lived in a house several streets over from the Thomas family. He and Heck were to remain good friends through the years. In 1910 after Senator Gore went to Washington, Heck received a letter from him reminding Heck they were "the same good old friends, true and tried, as when we slept on the grass and ate dirt together during the primeval days of Lawton."[22]

Heck soon decided to put down permanent roots in Lawton. On November 1, 1901, he purchased the west half of lots twenty-four and twenty-five, block one, for two hundred and twenty-five dollars. He built a new home there on what was then called South Boundary. The address later became known as 1114 Second Street.

Matie was delighted to have a house of her own. To most people, her new home might not look like much as far as houses went, but to her it was new and looked homey. It sported a raised roof, and for some reason, Heck painted the exterior a reddish brown color like that of a section hand's house.

Inside the house, there were three large rooms. First, came the living room with a woolen rug on the floor. A folding couch stood against one wall, and Matie and Heck's bed occupied a corner. Several chairs were grouped around an oblong oak table. Beyond the living room, one stepped into the girls' bedroom with its large chiffonier and beautiful bed with its high headboard, of which Matie was very proud. The kitchen stood at the back of the house. A lean-to shed adjoined it. Matie called this room her "summer kitchen" and equipped it with a coal oil cook stove.

The interior walls of the house were covered with fibre board. Matie tacked cheesecloth over the fibre board and papered the rooms. She planted lots of flowers in her yard. To some, the house might still appear a bit tacky, to Matie it was clean and comfortable, and she was a good housekeeper.

Matie hoped that someday she would be able to have a bigger and better house. Heck had built a few feet back on the lot with that idea in mind. But the day that he ordered a big barn be built at the back of the lot, Matie quit hoping. She knew she would never get another house.

Lawton was growing rapidly, demanding improvements as fast as it could obtain them. As Chief of Police of Lawton, Heck still carried his commission as U.S. deputy marshal. On February 10, 1902, Canada H. Thompson, the new U.S. marshal of the Western District, renewed Heck's commission.

The following month, city elections were again scheduled for permanent office holders. Heck was the only city official renominated by the Democrats. On April 3, he polled the heaviest vote in the city.[23] His heart swelled with pride. This proved to him that he had the confidence of the citizens of Lawton. Unknown to him then, that confidence was soon to tax him to the utmost.

Chapter 11

Fire Chief Thomas

The lack of an adequate water supply and a suitable fire department were two of the most desperate needs in Lawton during its earliest days. Peddlers hauled water from shallow wells and sold it all over town in barrels. No sewage system or proper sanitation facilities existed. A barrel of water stood before each business establishment as standard fire fighting equipment, along with a fifty-pound sack of salt. When the fire alarm (a shot fired in the air) sounded, everyone scampered to help in the fire line.

The town experienced its first big fire when but a few days old. On August 27, 1901, at 1:00 p.m., a blaze destroyed the livery barn of Hopkins Horse and Mule Market at 12 B Avenue. Three horses burned to death in the blaze. A bucket brigade prevented the fire from spreading to other nearby buildings. The loss was estimated at twelve hundred dollars.[1]

Soon after this, city officials called for a meeting to organize a volunteer fire brigade. Heck acted as fire chief in addition to being chief of police.[2]

Each water hauler was paid one dollar for making a run. Often twenty to thirty horses could be seen galloping toward the fire, creating a wild scene. Hundreds of volunteer fire fighters would descend upon the conflagration with buckets in

Heck Thomas served in dual capacity as Lawton's chief of police and fire chief. Courtesy Thomas Collection.

in hand. They soon extinguished the flames and pulled down walls with a grabhook to save the adjoining properties.[3]

Even so, one night in January 1902, the entire east block on Dove Street burned. The citizens clamored for better fire protection.

"The city council will have to answer to every citizen of Lawton for their negligence in providing some fire fighting apparatus," charged the editor of the Lawton *News*. "Get a chemical engine or two, or three, or four. The chance of a raging fire demands it."[4]

In response on February 3, 1902, the D.R. Volunteer Company, Lawton's first official fire department organized. Heck was appointed Fire Marshal in addition to his duties as Chief of Police. He chose twenty-six volunteer firemen to assist him. The city council passed an ordinance to pay the fire chief twelve dollars and fifty cents a month for his services. The firemen were to receive one dollar each for attending a fire and one dollar for each additional hour spent fighting the fire.[5]

Heck assessed his new fire department's needs and recommended the city purchase twelve rubber buckets and six fire axes at once.[6] These soon proved inadequate. On February 28, at 3:00 a.m., the town was again awakened by the cry of fire. Rushing to the scene with his fire department, Heck found the Palace Club Saloon on Avenue D, between Second and Third Streets, in flames. The south wind blew like a gale. The frame building burned as tinder, and the flames spread. Soon six buildings were gone, an estimated loss of $14,300.[7]

Heck knew the city could delay no longer. Officials ordered a light wagon with some chemicals, a ladder and other equipment costing twenty-five hundred dollars. When the new wagon arrived, it was placed in a sheet iron building across the street from the city hall.[8] When the fire alarm sounded, the first hack driver to get there, hitch his team to the wagon, and haul it to the fire would be paid five dollars.

Later, the fire department purchased a team of matched sorrels to make the run. Sleek, of medium build with heavy flowing manes and tails, the horses were beauties to behold and Heck was extremely proud of them. But one of the horses turned out bad and couldn't stand to make the runs. Subsequently, a big team of blacks was procured that served the fire department faithfully for a number of years.[9]

Heck continued to perform his duties as chief of police as effectively as he did that of fire chief. "No city in the United States of equal population can show a record for eight months that is more nearly clear of real crime than Lawton," boasted one newspaper editor. "This is an 'open' town, but thugs and criminals who occasionally land here find the atmosphere mighty uncongenial."[10]

Lawton grew steadily. Three school buildings had been built; more were needed. The volume of business at the post office was exceeded only by that at Guthrie and Oklahoma City. A telephone system had been established early in the spring. On May 10, 1902, the Lawton Confederate Veterans met at City Hall and organized the A.P. Hill Camp V.C.V. Heck was elected as First Lieutenant. On May 31, Memorial Day, he headed the town's first parade.

Heck shook his head when he read in the newspaper that day, that his youngest daughter, Beth, had died.[11] She had been very sick with measles. On a stormy night, the family had gone to the storm cellar and the measles had "gone in" on the child. But fortunately, she had not died and soon improved.

By July 1902, Lawton was well lit with forty arc streetlights scattered about the city. Dust still choked the unpaved streets, though, and there was much sickness from typhoid before city wells were dug. In late August, contracts for the new courthouse were let. On September 11, the first Frisco train whistled into town. That fall, the city staged a slightly delayed first birthday party. The celebration featured a bullfight with authentic Spanish toreador costumes, and a colorful Apache Indian dance by Fort Sill's most distinguished prisoner, Chief Geronimo.[12]

Heck enjoyed his new life and duties. But trouble always seemed to be lurking in the background. On the night of November 6, 1902, the new courthouse caught fire. While running to the scene, Heck seriously injured his left ankle.[13]

At first, he thought he had been shot, for there had been considerable shooting to alert everyone of the danger before the fire alarm bell rang. Heck thought a stray bullet might have struck his ankle. But he could find no bullet hole. Then he collapsed at the fire and had to be taken home. The doctor termed his injury a severe sprain. For several days, Heck remained close to his bed then went back to city hall.

Early in January 1903, Heck published a report as to how things had been going in police court. Since its beginning, sixteen hundred cases had been tried, collecting $5,920.75 in fines, with the greatest amount occurring in December, when $626.90 was taken in.[14]

"The amount of fines collected," noted the newspaper editor, "does not necessarily argue that Lawton has more than its share of the law breaking element. What it does argue is that the police force, with Heck Thomas as its chief, is ever watchful of the city's interests. Instead of money going dawn [sic] into police officers' pockets, as the case in many cities, it goes into the city treasury."[15] At the same time, Lawton did not have the reputation of being over zealous in police regulations, the editor added.

Heck did not believe in arresting a man just because he had too much to drink. The case of the farmer who came to town occasionally and proceeded to form "too intimate a connection with the bar fixtures" was frequently dismissed in police court. Knowing, too, those soldiers from nearby Fort Sill would not only have to settle with the city authorities, but all the authorities at the Fort if they missed roll call, the soldiers were frequently given wider latitude than they strictly deserved.

W.M. Murphy, who ran a saloon in Lawton at the time, recalled that when a man came into his establishment drunk, he made him sit down then sent for Heck. Usually the law officer took the man home.[16]

But Heck regularly locked up one old man in jail each Saturday night to sleep it off. About this time, Heck had obtained a little brown and white fox terrier which took up with the old man. Each Saturday night when Heck led the elderly fellow off to jail, the dog trailed after him. People laughed and said, "Well, there goes old so and so and Midge off to jail." The dog always spent the night in jail with the old chap.

The summer and fall of 1903 passed without too many problems in Lawton as Heck kept a tight rein on law and order. October 19, the fire department staged its first annual Fireman's Ball in the Akers Building. In spite of the inclement weather, about four hundred people attended the affair, for it was the first general dance held in Lawton. Stiffness and formality were out. The dancers swung gaily through the rhythms of the two-step, Virginia reel, the schottische, rye waltzes, and various quadrilles.[17]

The most "sensational event" of the evening reportedly was when Heck showed up wearing a standing collar. Some of his friends kidded that he had to be roped and tied hand and foot before Judge Blanding and Clerk Jacobs could button the restrictive cuff. Nevertheless, all agreed the collar was very becoming—even though Heck did look miserable in it.

Christmas that year was a time for more celebration. Lawton was now two years old, and Heck had established many good friendships. He invited the Hon. J.K.Tuttle, Colonel Hawkins, Charley Loux, Perry Foster, and Editor Frank Wright to eat Christmas dinner with his family.

"It was not exactly a function; bless you, no," Wright wrote afterwards. "It was a dinner to be eaten, to be laughed over, to be reveled in . . . to those whom Charley Loux calls a select few. The occasion was especially delightful to some who were there, because [they] rarely have the privilege to see the happiness of little children and to hear at this merry season of the year the laughter of baby lips. Had the hospitality of Mr. and Mrs. Thomas lacked this element, the gracious hours of the afternoon could not have passed with the sweetness that they did.

"Your dinner, Mrs. Thomas, was excellent and the abounding cheerfulness of your home was the thing which perhaps will be longest remembered . . . " Wright said.[18]

Winter passed and spring came. Heck was lulled into a sense of peace, but these days, unfortunately, trouble never seemed far away.

The threat of prairie fires was a constant danger to the homesteader on the plains. When the high, spring winds blew, the farmer was particularly watchful. But on the morning of March 2, 1904, Heck gave little thought to the matter. For that seemingly perfect day dawned balmy with a light southerly breeze. When Press Jones, of Mimms-Jones Barbershop on D Street, opened his shop, he found Heck waiting.[19]

"Going to be a beautiful day," Heck greeted him.

Press Jones agreed.

During the day, Heck could see fires burning on the distant mountains and the military reservation as the farmers burned their fields in the light breeze. Still, he saw no cause for alarm.

That night, about ten o'clock, all changed. The wind turned to the north with lightning swiftness. It blew with hurricane force. Heck saw the fires in the mountains suddenly becoming raging infernos impossible to control. The flames swept along for miles. Great rolling clouds of smoke obliterated the moon. It was impossible for anyone to face north, for the blowing sand and gravel cut their faces like needles. Burning embers and burning cow chips were hurled into the sky as the fire raced toward Lawton.[20]

"Wake up! Wake up!" Heck sounded the alarm. "The town's on fire!"

Hundreds of people rushed to North Boundary (now Gore Boulevard), and fought the fire with wet blankets and bran sacks and brooms. It seemed as if the whole town was doomed. Families evacuated their homes in the thick smoke and fled to Squaw Creek and the railroad. Here, waiting to flee, they stared in awe at the flames lighting the sky. Building after building caught fire. But oddly, the very wind which was the source of the trouble, was so strong that it blew out the flames almost as soon as they started. Only a few outbuildings were destroyed, but the danger continued.

As fire chief, Heck had the seemingly impossible task of stopping the flames as well as that of giving police orders. He determined to make a fire break one hundred feet wide along North Boundary. He ordered every available man and all the water possible to the front. Wagons dashed back and forth carrying water from wells in the northeast part of the city and from ponds. Mayor Turner and Heck walked up and down the fire line encouraging the fire fighters. Heck ordered his police officers to be on the lookout for looters as so many citizens had left their homes in sudden flight.

Heck thought he could hold the line if the wind didn't shift. Several times the flames drove the fire fighters back. Heck knew they were finished if the fire jumped North Boundary. Debris flew in the air. Trash piled up along fences and caught fire. Heck established a second line of fire fighters along the fences. Afterwards, observers said this action on Heck's part saved the city. The sight of him vigorously fighting the fire, though older than many of them, stirred the fire fighters onward in the stifling thick clouds of smoke and heat.

Suddenly, the air cooled and blew out of the west. The fire fighters cheered for they knew the tide had turned in their favor. The wind moderated. The flames began to flicker out. By dawn, the big fire was over. In relief, the fire fighters sank to the street to rest.

"They performed a miracle," Heck told the mayor. "I know you will tell them so."

Lawton citizens cheered, laughed, and wept when the flames were out. They returned to their homes to clean up the mess. They found sand piled in fence corners like snowdrifts and their houses full. Wash tubs and wash boilers were found blocks away.[21]

That spring, the citizens of Lawton remained extremely conscious concerning fire. Heck urged the city council to provide a better source of water for fire fighting and more fire equipment. But before this could happen, another situation commmanded his attention.

Chapter 12

Colonel Hawkins' Ordeal

Lawton, it seemed, was always in political upheaval. That year of 1904 was no different. But this time it was to have a serious consequence that Heck's family was to long remember.

The trouble developed between Col. Will Hawkins, Heck's first assistant chief of police, and T.A. Russell. Russell had founded the *State Democrat,* which had begun publishing at the opening of Lawton.[1] After one term as assistant chief of police, Hawkins moved on to serve as Sergeant at Arms in the Oklahoma Legislature. Now he held mining interests. At the Lawton townsite opening, Hawkins and Russell had shared a tent as friends.[2] But bad blood now existed between the two men.

Afterward, Russell claimed the difficulty had begun about a year before when Hawkins was refused a place on Lawton's second police force. Hawkins held Russell responsible for his rejection. Sometime after Hawkins was out of office, Russell had printed a "scurrilous defamation of character"[3] about Hawkins which "could not be justified under any circumstances but especially as he was no longer a police officer."[4] Heated words passed between the two men. Each was warned the other was "out to get him."

Hawkins had long since shown he was a reformed character from his gambling days. Children loved and trusted him. Hosts of the little adorers surrounded him when he was seated and hovered about him in a convoy when he walked. In passing, he never failed to greet one. Courtesy was the essence of his character. Wells Fargo Express Co., for whom he had worked in Cripple Creek, Colorado, had given him the highest recommendation.[5]

When urged to make the miscreant, Russell, suffer, Colonel Hawkins replied, "I can afford to obey the law."[6] He wanted no revenge.

"But then, what would one expect of a Georgian and a gentleman?" asked the Lawton *Constitution.*[7]

Russell soon proved he was not so gallant. The trouble came to a head just before noon on election day, April 4, a month following the big fire.

The sidewalk before city hall was filled with people on both sides of the various political issues, clustered in groups, arguing and working for their candidates. In one of these groups stood Hawkins and Russell, both Democrats. One made a remark that started the trouble. Witnesses said Hawkins then pushed or knocked Russell from the sidewalk and followed him to the street. Whereon, Russell pulled his Colt .45.[8]

Witnesses later testified that Hawkins retreated backwards in the street, begging Russell not to shoot in the crowd, for fear of hitting someone else.[9]

But Russell threw off three shots at a distance not exceeding fifteen feet. One shot took effect in the fleshy part of Hawkins' right leg, one in his left knee, and the third one entered the left side of his abdomen. By then, Hawkins had drawn his gun. He got in position to shoot. Russell got behind a man and dodged so Hawkins could not fire without endangering others. Then Russell took shelter behind a wagon and team. He started from this to the stairway leading over the Lowery Barbershop. Hawkins fired one shot which went wild. Russell stopped in the stairway and fired another shot which also went wild.[10] Hawkins then fell from the effect of his wounds. Bystanders rushed to his side and assisted him to a room.

Chief Thomas and his men arrested Russell and lodged him in the county jail. But feeling ran high against the editor. Heck spirited Russell from the town to Fort Sill.

Because there was no hospital in Lawton, Heck moved Hawkins, his friend, to his own home. For more than a week, Hawkins lay in Beth and Harley's big bed, mortally wounded, while Matie cared for him. He was a good-looking man, thirty-seven-years-old and engaged to a woman by the name of Marie A. Dean. Daily, the inquiry in general was "What is the latest from Col. Hawkins?"[11]

Hawkins' stock had risen "above par" with the public for his act of bravery which possibly saved the lives of innocent people in the area when the shooting occurred.[12] A resolution signed by thirty-two citizens commended him for his "noble acts and regard for innocent human life in as much that you refused to fire at your antagonist, when by your doing so you might have injured an innocent person . . . ."[13]

For five days, Hawkins lay in critical condition. On Saturday he seemed to rally, and it was thought chances for his recovery were reversed.[14] On Monday, the doctors were even more hopeful. But that night, Hawkins took a turn for the worst. When Matie gave him his medicine for the last time, he uttered, "I thank you, I thank you." These were the last words he spoke.[15]

At four a.m., Hawkins moved his head from one side to the other, threw his long limbs out, raised himself by a mighty effort, and fell back dead.[16]

Hawkins' funeral was held two days later. It was the largest ever held in Lawton up to that time, and the sorrow was "one of the most general felt." The procession was one mile in length, and the city hall bell tolled for one hour.

As the funeral car neared the graveyard, a messenger overtook it. Colonel Hawkins' brother had arrived from Georgia, said the messenger. Hold the burial. Mr. Hawkins subsequently took his brother's body back to Georgia to be buried.[17]

Before leaving Lawton, Mr. Hawkins asked to see his brother's murderer in the Fort Sill jail. He gazed a long time at Russell as if trying to memorize his features.

Russell was brought to trial for the murder of Colonel Hawkins that December. But the deputy sheriff and Mayor Turner were strong advocates in his defense, and Russell was acquitted.

Russell left immediately for the East where he started another newspaper. One day, news came that he was murdered. It was never known by whom. Heck always believed it was by Colonel Hawkins' brother.

In appreciation for Matie taking care of Hawkins, Marie A. Dean, his financee, gave her a fine water color which she had painted. After this, life in Lawton seemed to settle down for a time, but new storm clouds hovered on the horizon.

Chapter 13

Calm Before the Storm

That spring of 1905 began peacefully enough for Heck. Construction on the new city hall was progressing rapidly. The population of Lawton now numbered about four thousand people. To provide water for the growing city, workers were laying an eleven-mile, sixteen-inch gravity transmission line from an earthen and wooden dam in the Wichita Mountains north of Lawton. Besides furnishing drinking water, Heck knew this would also greatly improve the city's fire fighting capabilities.

If that wasn't enough good news, He learned President Teddy Roosevelt was coming to town. He was to arrive on April 9 for a wolf hunt on the "Big Pasture," which was located on the Comanche Reservation.[1] Roosevelt had heard stories about John Abernathy, a local cowboy, who had furnished more than one thousand wolves to zoos across the nation. Abernathy captured these wolves by riding his horse alongside a fleeing wolf, then leaping onto the animal's back as a bulldogger would, and jamming his gloved fist into the wolf's mouth. After this, he tied the wolf's jaw shut. President Roosevelt had heard about Abernathy and wanted to view his amazing "bring 'em back alive" wolf hunting technique for himself.

Heck and other local law officers joined forces with soldiers from Fort Sill in setting up stiff security measures for the president's protection. Heck's daughter, Beth, remembered one story he delighted in telling about this event.

When the President's train arrived, the security force immediately surrounded it to safeguard the president and to hold back the pressing crowd. In the crowd was one old black man whose political views differed radically from those of Roosevelt. On spotting Heck and his men, the old Negro excitedly exclaimed to those near him: "See there! I told you he was a crook. The police already have him in custody."

Roosevelt was so impressed by Abernathy's wolf-hunting performance that shortly after his three-day visit to the Big Pasture, he appointed Abernathy as Deputy U.S. Marshal of the Southern District.

That spring of 1905 was election time, too. Heck handily won reelection, showing he still held the trust and confidence of the people. Indeed, Heck was a most popular fellow in Lawton. Almost everyone there fondly referred to him as "Uncle Heck." With his kind, courteous manners, one would never guess he possessed a will of steel. Now in his mid-fifties, he was still a handsome man. Grey-haired from the time his youngest daughter could remember, he never seemed like an old man to her.

On the other hand, to Beth, her mother never seemed young. Matie cooked and kept house. She milked the family's Jersey cow, made cottage cheese, and sold milk and butter. The Thomas family lived at the end of town, on South Boundary, and kept their cow staked to a long rope in the pasture there. Once, the cow got her rope tangled around Matie's foot and Matie fell, injuring herself. Pregnant at the time, she lost the baby and couldn't have any more children.

Theodore Roosevelt and group of noted west Texans on famous wolf hunt in April 1905. Left to right standing: Lee "A.W." Bivens, Capt. Bill McDonald, Jack Abernathy, Maj. A.B. Young, Capt. S. Burkeburnett, President Roosevelt, E.M. Gillis. Sitting: Two soldiers, Bonnie More, Chief Quanah Parker (on his knees), Cecil Lyons, Dr. Lambert, and D.P. "Phy" Taylor. Courtesy Western History Collections, University of Oklahoma Library.

Following her accident, Matie put on considerable weight. If this bothered Heck, he never mentioned it to her, Beth said, though he was always fastidious about his own appearance.

On his fifty-fifth birthday, Heck enjoyed hearing the crowd at city hall try to guess his age.[2] He would never admit to being more than forty-one. He insisted that was as old as he was going to get.

He kept those at city hall laughing with his wry sense of humor and witty songs. He was always pulling a prank on someone. Once his barber, Press Jones, got even when Heck learned that Matie's sister, Annie, was coming from Tulsa for a visit.

Annie was now a widow. One day in 1895, a drunken Indian had come into Jeff Archer's furniture and hardware store and demanded whiskey. Archer tried to convince him he didn't have any. The Indian fired his gun. The bullet struck a barrel of gunpowder which exploded. The Indian was killed outright. Archer suffered a concussion and died several days later. At the time, Annie was pregnant and the mother of two small children. Archer left her economically well off.

Heck had always liked Annie. He wanted to look nice for her visit. He went to Jones' barbershop to have his mustache singed (a fashion of the time.) Heck had pulled many a prank on Jones. This time, Jones decided he would fix Heck up good. He put something on Heck's hair and mustache that turned them an "ungodly color" according to Beth. When they tried to wash it out, it left Heck's grey locks pink. Whether that recipe for hair dye in the back of one of Heck's old day books had anything to do with Annie's visit that time, Beth never knew. But she was certain her father wouldn't have wanted Annie seeing him with pink hair and mustache. He took too much pride in his appearance for that.

Once Matie's parents came to visit. The Reverend and Mrs. Mowbray had moved to Choctaw, Oklahoma Territory, in 1891. Following Jeff Archer's death, they returned to Tulsa. Reverend Mowbray gave up preaching to handle Annie's business affairs. Also, he obtained a mortician's license and opened the Mowbray Funeral Home in Tulsa, which he ran with the assistance of his son, George, who had ridden posse for Heck in Guthrie.

Heck never cared for Reverend Mowbray, Beth said, but he was always polite to him. This time when her grandfather and grandmother came to visit, Beth kept hearing her father call her grandfather "Lord Mowbray." This puzzled Beth. She asked her mother, why did her father keep doing that? He was just making fun of him, Matie said, teasing Beth's grandfather about being a descendant of Lord Mowbray of England.

Heck loved to have company. His Southern upbringing had taught him to be very hospitable. He had many friends in Lawton. Often they came to visit, or to bring him wild game to eat, knowing how much he loved it.

Al Jennings came sometimes, too. But he was never one of Heck's favorites. Redhaired and nasty-looking, as far as Beth was concerned, Jennings had quit outlawing and gone to preaching. There was room for change, she reasoned, but she didn't think he made it. When she and Harley were young, Jennings would try to catch them and kiss them. If her father had known this, Beth was sure he would have killed him. "Yeah, I know he would've," she said.

Sometimes, Heck sent to Galveston where he used to live and ordered oysters in the shell to be shipped by train. Down by the barn, he built a coal fire and placed a wire screen over it, on which to broil the oysters. He invited his friends to a stag dinner.

To Beth, her father was a fascinating man and she absolutely adored him. Whenever she saw him coming down the road, she would say, "Here comes Heck!" and run to meet him so she could ride in the buggy and be with him by herself.

Those days, neither Heck nor Matie attended church. Heck had lost interest in organized religion long ago, and Matie's father had been too strict for her and she had dropped out of church too. Neither of their parents objected to Harley and Beth going to church though and Heck would sit around and sing religious songs to them. Beth was confident her father was a Christian.

As far as she knew, Heck's one besetting sin was that he fought game chickens. Where he picked up this interest, Beth didn't know. It may have been in Georgia, or it may have been from Bill Tilghman for he shared this interest.

However he came by it, many a Saturday afternoon, a group of men with their fancy roosters met by Heck's fenced chicken pen at the back of his barn to stage their chicken fights. At this time, Matie always herded Harley and Beth into the house. Chicken fighting didn't seem like a good sport to her for it was a fight to the death and bloody, but Heck was enthusiastic about the game.

He took much interest in his game chickens. He exercised his roosters on a long bench to make their legs strong, placing his hands beneath their wings and lifting the birds up and down, and backwards and forward. He cooked meat for the chickens, ground it up, and added other ingredients. He put sharp, wicked-looking gaffs over the roosters' spurs before a fight.

As far as Beth knew, her father never gambled on his chickens. He set hens and raised some chickens and sold some. Once in awhile, he bought a fancy rooster off some-

Heck Thomas with his game chickens in 1911, near the end of his life. Courtesy Thomas Collection.

place. He was very proud of his chickens. They were a pretty breed, russet brown with different markings, smaller than the usual chicken. Their meat was very tasty. Occasionally, Heck would let Matie have one of his game hens to eat, but nobody killed one of his beautiful roosters.

Matie did not fuss at Heck about his game chickens, but she wanted to raise some Plymouth Rocks to eat. One day, she set some eggs under a hen in the barn. Heck threw a fit. He didn't want those common Plymouth Rocks around his fancy chickens.

Beth helped Heck feed his chickens. She fed the horse and the cow. The only thing that scared her was that sometimes at night when they returned from somewhere, her father would ask her to climb into the hay mow and throw down a couple of flakes of hay for the horse. Beth was afraid to go up there, for the railroad track ran only a mile from their house, across the pasture. The hobos liked to gather under a bridge there and do their cooking. Sometimes the hobos would come to their house and Matie always fed them. Beth was afraid that when she climbed into the hay mow one of the hobos might be sleeping there. Heck would assure her, "You don't need to worry. I'm right here." So, in spite of being scared, Beth would do as he asked.

Sometimes their family went camping, usually just Heck, Harley, and Beth. Matie did not care much for going out and spending the night. But Heck loved getting into the open again. He would drive them down to Cache Creek in the buggy. There they slept on the ground. Harley and Beth put on old dresses and played in the water. Heck showed them how to cook bacon on a crooked stick held over the fire. Occasionally, Heck drove the girls to Mt. Scott, or they climbed Signal Mountain to scratch their names in the little roofless building there. Other times, he took them to the Comanche reservation to visit the Indians.

Once Chris Madsen, whose wife had died, and his son Reno went camping with Heck, Harley, and Beth. Reno warmed a can of Pork and Beans as part of their dinner. Beth considered them the best beans she had ever eaten, and couldn't understand why her mother's beans never tasted like this.

Heck and Madsen had a good time that trip, laughing and talking about all the experiences they had been through together. They told of wild rides across moonlit prairies, fierce fights with desperate criminals, and dangerous passages of swollen streams. They related anecdotes of late lamented friends and notorious rogues. Like all men who have scented the smoke of battle, Beth recalled they were modest and passed over their narrow escapes with a shrug.

Heck teased Madsen about the time Chief Whirlwind of the Cheyennes, Madsen's bosom friend, died and left his squaws and daughters to Madsen. The ungrateful lawman never did claim his rights under the terms of Chief Whirlwind's will. In return for Heck's ribbing, Madsen teased him about being "Scissortail."

The two men chuckled over the time they crossed a river in the Territory in a buggy. Madsen dropped his buggy whip. The water was shallow, but Madsen didn't want to get his feet wet. Heck said, "Well, Chris, just put your foot on the hub of that wheel and you can reach it."

Just as Madsen got situated, Heck pulled the horses up a little. A round, portly fellow, Madsen plunged headlong into the water. The first thing he said after he dug the weeds from his eyes was, "See what you done, Heck!"[3]

The stories went on long into the night, while Harley, Reno, and Beth listened by the light of the flickering campfire.

Harley, l., and Beth Thomas, Heck's youngest children, loved going camping with their father. Courtesy Thomas Collection.

Heck and Madsen remembered a time in 1894 when they were chasing outlaws in Osage country. They had three Creek half-breeds along as aids.[4] While tramping the hills, they flushed out a trio of whiskey peddlers and interrupted their outlaw search to give chase. About dark, they ran the whiskey peddlers into a ravine. Heck and Madsen stationed themselves at the mouth of the gully and directed the Indians to post themselves at the head.

"We've got them bottled up and we'll get them in the morning," Madsen said. "You see that they don't get away and when we get them, we'll give you a drink of the whiskey." He knew this promise would insure the necessary vigilance of the Indians.

About two a.m., one of the Indians woke Heck and Madsen. "We want to go down and get those fellows now," the Indian said.

"What's the matter?" Madsen asked. "Are you afraid they'll get away?"

"No," the Indian said, "but we had a talk and we want to get them now."

Heck and Madsen argued that the men were armed and had the advantage of night that they had better wait until morning. Then they could take them easily.

The Indian returned to his companions. In a few minutes he returned. "We had another talk and we want to get them now," he spoke firmly.

"And take the chance of getting killed?" Heck asked in disbelief.

"That's all right," the Indian replied without concern. "There are three of them. There are three of us. We figure they won't kill more than two of us. This'll leave one of us to drink the whiskey."

Against the advice of Heck and Madsen, but with their consent, the three Indians swept down from their hiding place to where the whiskey peddlers were resting around their campfire. They captured the three law breakers without an exchange of gunshots. When Heck and Madsen reached the scene, the three whiskey peddlers were in handcuffs and the three Indians gulping away at the confiscated whiskey.

Heck and Madsen spoke solemnly of the danger in being a U.S. deputy marshal. Madsen related that during the time he was at Guthrie sixty deputies or possemen had been killed. He said they never had the crepe off the door. Heck stated that his first three deputies had been killed.

"The next man who asked for the job, I refused," he said.[5] "I was getting superstitious then."

Sometimes Bill Tilghman came to visit Heck and his family. Tilghman's first wife had died, leaving him with three children. He, too, laughed about old times with Heck.

They told about the day two of them were sitting in a Guthrie cafe eating. Heck noticed Tilghman kept giving the waitress the eye, but he didn't say anything to her. After the two men left the cafe, Heck got some woman to call Tilghman. She made a date to meet him by the courthouse. Tilghman went there at the time he was supposed to and walked up and down. When it was beginning to look as if he was growing impatient and about to leave, Heck stepped out of the shrubbery. Chagrined, Tilghman said, "Heck, I'm gonna kill you!" In retaliation, the next time it rained, he fixed Heck's hat so all the water overflowed the brim and down his neck.

Heck was always kind to animals. He owned a beautiful horse, a fine looking animal that had once been a race horse. The family had two dogs, the brown and white fox terrier named Midge that a cousin in Tulsa had sent Harley and Beth. Beth never got attached to this dog. Her favorite was Sport, a fair-sized, dark brown mongrel.

Beth and Harley's bedroom had an outside door. In cold weather, the dogs slept in a shed. But sometimes Harley and Beth would hear Sport scratching at their door and let him in. He shot past them, and went to the foot of their bed. This aggravated Matie for she had to wash those dirty sheets on the scrub board.

That spring when Beth was five-years-old, the city dog catcher came to the Thomas home and tried to capture Sport, thinking he was a stray. Each time he got the rope on the dog, Beth grabbed it and took it off. Heck was home and he chanced to look out the window and saw what was happening. He came outside with his gun and told the dog catcher he had one minute to get that rope off that dog and get off the place.

John Lantznester, a close friend of Heck's and a Confederate veteran, laughed about the dog catcher incident for years. He said an old Negro named Ellison, working around the place for Heck, had seen the whole thing. He told Lantznester later, "Mr. John, that pistol looked as long as my arm, and I guess it looked that way to the dog catcher, cause he had that rope off and he was gone in less than half a minute."[6]

Those days, Harley and Beth were both quite thin. Harley was of dark complexion resembling Heck, with his brown eyes and hair. Beth's hair and eyes were brown, too, but lighter than Harley's. She looked more like Matie, but she never felt as close to her mother as she did to her father.

Heck often thought of his other family. He received letters from Henry, Albert, and Belle and wrote to them in return. But Albert was always the one to whom he felt the closest. Albert now worked for a railway company in Florida. Each year at harvest time he sent Heck and Matie a box of oranges and a box of kumquats.

As the spring of 1905 continued, Heck seemed quite content. During the April election, the citizens of Lawton, seeing the need for an improved form of government for their growing city, had approved a charter and commission form of government. After reorganization, Dick Jones, the new mayor, turned Heck down cold on the customary courtesy of suggesting names for appointment to the police force. He also appointed a new fire chief, relieving Heck of his duties here.[7] L.M. Radley, had come to Lawton highly recommended with service on fire departments in Kansas and elsewhere.[8]

But Radley's appointment didn't come soon enough. One night before the new fire chief took over, Heck was running to fight a blaze above Cumming's Furniture Store on E Avenue and he fell. The consequences were to prove tragic.

Chapter 14

The Declining Years

At first, it was thought Heck had suffered a heart attack while running to the fire. He lay in bed for several weeks with Matie hovering anxiously over him. He recuperated slowly, and his friends drifted in and out, wishing him well.

As soon as he was able to get back on his feet, though still weak, Heck insisted on going back to work. His family had no other income but his salary as chief of police. He promised Matie he would take things a little easier, but he was never really well after that.

During the summer of 1905, Heck's son Albert came from Florida to visit for a week and stayed a month. That helped Heck's morale a great deal. Soon he seemed to be pretty much his old self and was back to pulling his pranks at city hall.

In September, he gave two men, who were going to a Knights of Phythias district meeting in Altus, a note to deliver to the sheriff there.[1] After the sheriff received the note, he asked the two Lawtonians if they knew what it said. "No," each replied. "Well," said the sheriff, "it's a note telling me to arrest you." Heck's two old friends realized Heck had got the best of them once again. It took some fast talking for them to talk the sheriff out of that one. Of course, Heck soon heard about it.

Two weeks later, Heck surprised the officials of the District Court with a midnight supper at the opera house. Following the evening show, he served them fried chicken, salad, and cake. He boasted that this "fully substantiates" his position of the superiority of the flavor of game chickens.[2]

In October, the new city hall was completed. It was a fine looking, two-story, red brick building located at 311-313 Fourth Avenue. Heck happily moved police headquarters into new quarters in a corner of the full basement. Fire Chief Radley and the fire department, with a one-bay station, took possession of another corner.

By October 18, Heck seemed well enough that Matie felt it safe for her and the two girls to travel to Tulsa on the train to spend a month visiting Grandmother Mowbray.[3]

Not long after their return to Lawton in November, Mayor Dick Jones announced the reorganization of the city fire department. He dispensed with the volunteer firemen and appointed a paid fire department.

Heck attended the last meeting of the Lawton volunteer fire department on December 14, 1905.[4] The organization's property and cash assets were inventoried and handed over to the treasurer, who donated the fire chief's buggy to Heck. The organization disbanded. Several nights later, the new Lawton fire department organized and elected an assistant fire chief to help Chief Radley.[5] Mayor Jones sold the volunteer fire department's fine team of horses and purchased a larger team of blacks in Fort Worth.[6] Reportedly, the old team was sold to a railway dray company. But each time the horses heard a bell clanging, they took off running and had to be retired.

On his fifty-sixth birthday in January 1906, Heck felt fairly well, still keeping the crowd at city hall entertained. His witticisms often found their way into the newspaper, such as

The old city hall in Lawton. The "x" in the lower left corner marks the office of Heck Thomas, Chief of Police. **Courtesy Thomas Collection.**

this one, which one reporter wrote about for the amusement of his readers in the Lawton *News Republican*:[7]

> "Heck spoke of a certain fellow as being associated with 'mining circles.' Those who were listening at city hall shook their heads. 'The fellow,' they corrected, 'is nothing but a poor prospector.' 'But,' responded Heck, 'Your perception and my perception of the term "mining circles" is different. The man spent all his time digging little holes. Those are circles. Therefore, the man is clearly associated with mining circles.'"

"No one could argue with his logic," noted the reporter.

Shortly after that, Heck's illness struck again. He lay critically ill for "some weeks." His doctor sent him to St. Anthony's Hospital in Oklahoma City. Medical specialists diagnosed his problem as a ruptured mitral valve, received the night he fell while running to his last fire. His weakened body had also developed a kidney ailment. Today, doctors could have operated and easily repaired the damage to his heart, but then they could do little but send him home.

While he lay in bed, dozens of Heck's friends came to see him, including Bill Tilghman.[8] Heck's oldest son, Henry, came to visit, too. Like Albert, Henry was dark and good-looking, appearing more like his father than any of Heck's other children.

The latter part of June, Heck rallied enough to make his way back to his desk as chief of police.[9] A person of lesser stamina might have succumbed to this double onslaught to his health, but not Heck. But even seven-year-old Beth could listen to her father's heart "chug," and know it was not right.

If Heck's illness wasn't enough for Matie to contend with, she had Beth to care for that summer, too. Beth had missed the entire school year because of a consistent, low grade fever.

Now, she was down to "skin and bones." No one knew what was wrong with her.

Though never feeling well himself, Heck did his best to entertain the sick child. Sometimes he would do little things to make Beth laugh, like slipping into the summer kitchen where Matie had her cream rising on the milk and snitching each of them a bite. This way he could coax her into eating a bit, too.

One morning that fall when Beth awoke, she found she no longer had a fever. She got out of bed and told her parents, "Well, now I can go to school." She did.

In November 1906, Heck was pleased to hear that the mayor had relieved Fire Chief L.M. Radley of his duties for "physical condition unfitting him for his position."[10] People had been complaining about Radley's drinking for a year. On December 26, the mayor appointed Sim Sheppard in Radley's place.[11]

That winter, Heck's health took another setback. This time, doctors diagnosed his problem as Bright's Disease, compounded by the kidney ailment and heart problem. The cold wind blew around the small house at Second and Boundary Street with a mournful sound as Heck kept to his bed.

By March 1907, Heck felt confident enough in his ability to regain his health that he again announced his candidacy for reelection as chief of police. He made his statement short and to the point:[12]

> "TO MY DEMOCRATIC FRIENDS. Several years ago in running to a fire on E. Avenue, over Cumming's Furniture Store, I over-exerted myself and dilated some part of my heart structure. For a long time, I was in critical condition—am much better now, but too weak to see all my friends. So I hope they will read this and consider themselves called on to register before next

Saturday night, when registration closes. Then they can all vote for me at the primary election March 7."

The editor of the Lawton *Enterprise* added that any comment the *Enterprise* might make in regard to Heck's candidacy "would not come in the way of news matter, but rather in the form of testimony to the merits of a man beloved of his neighbors and friends, and known throughout the Southwest as one of the most honest and efficient officers whoever followed the track of an outlaw. Heck Thomas is a true democrat, a faithful servant of the public, and a man among his fellows. If the democrats in their wisdom see fit to again honor him by nominating him to the office of City Marshal he will be elected by one of his usual majorities."

Heck was nominated in the primary election that year on the Democrat ticket. But in the March general election, he barely creaked by his Republican opponent, T.S. Walker, with a mere majority of three votes.[13] This lack of public confidence in his health was readily apparent to Heck and left him feeling despondent.

Heck's closest friends, however, stood staunchly by him. One Saturday, a number of them gathered at city hall where they proudly presented him with a beautiful gold badge with a diamond in the center. An old friend of Heck's and conductor on the Colorado, Oklahoma, and Gulf Railroad did the honor of pinning the badge to his shirt. Printed upon the face of the badge in black enamel were these words: "City Marshal Heck Thomas."[14]

Wrote the editor of the *Enterprise*:[15]

> "Few men living have been presented with more medals and emblems of esteem than this invincible hero, Heck Thomas, and very, very few men could receive all

the admiration and love that has been heaped upon him without, to use a slang expression, 'getting the big head' a little bit. But no such man is 'Our Heck.' Modest, unassuming and gentlemanly conduct are his prevailing characteristics, and no man, be he great or small, rich or poor, but receives the kindest treatment at his hands. Long may you live, friend Heck, and 'may the happiest days of your past be the saddest of your future,' this is the wish of this writer."

Justifiably, Heck was heartbroken the day he lost the badge which his friends had presented that eventful day. He and his family searched for it everywhere. Then one morning, when Harley and Beth were raking out the old hay in the cow lot, Beth found the badge. Heck was "tickled to death" over its recovery.

Regardless of the lack of confidence of the public in his regaining his health, Heck was back at his desk by June 1. In his public report of June 13, 1907, he summed up the activities of the police department again.[16] His officers had made 6,038 arrests since August 1901. Though Lawton was growing rapidly, Heck noted that the yearly total of arrests was going down. He believed the lawless element, which was always attendant in a new country, no longer existed in Lawton, thanks to his effective five-man police force. In conjunction with all of these arrests by the police department, the city court had collected more than thirty thousand dollars in small sums and fines. There had never been a dispute over even as much as five cents of that amount.

The first of November, Mayor Jones' austere budget forced the police staff to work longer hours. Heck went to work at eight a.m. and did not get off until ten p.m. Assistant Chief John Lantznester had the eight p.m. to eight a.m. shift. Joe Edward and the other two officers on the police force worked ten-hour shifts each.[17] These long hard hours did not help Heck's health, but he did not complain.

On November 16, 1907, came one of the proudest moments of Heck's life: Oklahoma was admitted as a state to the union by President Teddy Roosevelt. Heck had done perhaps as much as anyone in bringing this about. He had fought personally to bring law and order out of the early chaos that existed in the crime-infested Twin Territories. Some of the Confederate veterans in Lawton planned to attend the statehood ceremonies in Guthrie.[18] Heck wanted very much to go, but did not get to do so because of his health and his job.

With the extermination of the outlaw gangs in the Twin Territories, the work of the United States marshals had dwindled to small cases and routine matters. With statehood, except for offenses committed in violation of federal laws, law enforcement in Oklahoma was now turned over to the local police and sheriff departments. This extra work added to the burden of Heck's duties. But he handled his work as efficiently and honestly as ever.

As a case in point, his daughter, Harley, remembered an incident that happened about that time. She, her mother, and Beth had driven downtown in the buggy with Heck. A man, who was about to go to jail on some charge, stopped them on the street. Heck got down from the buggy to see what he wanted. The man tried to bribe Heck with a hundred dollars to drop the charge against him. Heck stood there waiting until the fellow got through talking, then he hauled off and knocked him down. This was his way of saying he did not take bribes.

Beth remembered another incident even more frightening. Another man in town had been up to something, and Heck had caught him at it. The crook vowed he was going to kill Heck and demanded a meeting that night on South Boundary to shoot it out. At that time, Lawton had city street lights, but on South Boundary, it was "dark for blocks and blocks" before one reached the city proper. Also, because of his bad health, Heck could no longer draw his gun as fast as he once did. Matie, Harley, and Beth were frightened. They cried and begged him not to go.

Heck pleaded for understanding. "Can't you see? I've got to go. I can't back down from it. I can't let him think he can order me around like that."

So, he took his gun in hand. He told Matie to tie a paper sack around his wrist. He cocked the hammer of his firearm inside the paper sack and left the house. Fortunately, the other man did not show up that night. Otherwise, he might have received more than he bargained for, according to Beth.

During the summer of 1907, Heck played a part in a movie. It had all begun in the spring of 1905 when President Roosevelt had come to the Big Pasture on his famous wolf hunt. John R. Abernathy, the Frederick cowboy who had been the president's principal guide and wolf chaser, had gained the president's admiration by his "bring 'em back alive" technique. Subsequently, Roosevelt had named Abernathy as U.S. deputy marshal in the Southern District, then in February 1907, U.S. marshal at Guthrie, in spite of Abernathy's friendship with Al Jennings, the reformed outlaw.

The trouble was, back East, nobody believed the president when he boasted of Abernathy's wolf-catching skills. Abernathy took affront at this. He wanted to prove to the nation that it was so. He realized that the new field of motion pictures was the way to do this.

W.E. Curtis of Kansas City had invented a suitable camera. Organizing the Oklahoma Mutoscope Company with a capital stock of fifty thousand dollars, Abernathy engaged Curtis to film his wolf catching feat.[19] Assembling a crew, which included a photographer and Chris Madsen, who was now Abernathy's chief deputy at Guthrie, Abernathy and Curtis set off with their families for the Wichita Mountains in southern Oklahoma, near Cache.

Soon, Abernathy saw he did not have the expertise to produce the film, "Wolf Hunt." Two weeks after the start of production, he sent for Bill Tilghman, who was living on his ranch near Chandler. Tilghman had no experience in film making either, but Abernathy insisted that he knew "how to get things done."[20]

Abernathy put Tilghman in full charge of the film project. Tilghman saw at once they needed more than the wolf catching incident in the film and suggested they weave it into a story about a gang of outlaws robbing a bank, a scenario with which he was well familiar. To make the story, "The Bank Robbery," more realistic, Tilghman hired Al Jennings to play the part of the king of the outlaw band that was supposed to rob the Cache bank. He hired Heck, who, along with Tilghman and Madsen, led the posse as Jennings fled into the mountains. So, The Three Guardsmen rode again. Chief Quannah Parker appeared in the film, too. During the filming of the story, Tilghman strived to make it as authentic as possible.

Proud of their finished film, in February 1909, Tilghman and Abernathy took it to Washington to show to the president. Roosevelt held a special screening for "The Bank Robbery" in the East Room of the White House. President Roosevelt was so impressed by the amateur film makers' accomplishment that he arranged for the trio to stay in Washington and help photograph the inauguration of the new incoming president, William Howard Taft.[21]

Further, President Roosevelt issued a special order for the Oklahomans to attend the Army-Navy reception, which was the last of the brilliant social functions of the Roosevelt administration. It was a great honor for civilians to be invited to this. The occasion demanded silk top hats and tails. Madsen and Tilghman couldn't resist having their picture taken while all duded up. They titled the picture "Before the Ball."[22] They had a second photo taken in tattered coats and mashed hats which they called "After the Ball."[23] They sent both pictures to Heck.

Heck chuckled over the pictures, especially the one of his two old friends in top hat and tails. In mock indignation, he told a local reporter that in his book, Madsen and Tilghman were "outlawed." He claimed they had both "wandered off the range" and wound up in Washington, where they had got "locoed eating strange weeds along the Potomac."[24]

Heck was quoted as saying in his best Southern drawl, "I wipes my hands of 'em, suh! They jes' kain't throw in with my outfit from this time on, an' I swar, if they come loafin' down the trail an' hit my camp about chuck time, thar'll be nothin' doin'."

On April 3, 1909, the Lawton *Constitution* announced Heck's candidacy for his fifth term as city marshal, "Heck Thomas Puts Out His Platform." Heck stated the facts briefly and to the point:[25]

> "My Platform: Treat everybody right. My record: Faithful to every trust that has ever been reposed in me."

He summed up his thirty-year record in breaking up some of the worst gangs in Texas, Arkansas, and Oklahoma, including the Bass, Dalton, and Doolin gangs, risking his life and enduring all sorts of hazardous exposure and other hardships. "Have been wounded six times in performance of my duties, but have never had a personal difficulty in my life," he stated. He concluded his notice of candidacy by reminding the citizens that during his time in office in Lawton, thousands of dollars had been collected in fees, "and there has never been a dollar short in this office."

The *Constitution* editor endorsed Heck saying that the man, woman, or child who did not know "Uncle Heck" did not know Lawton. His "manly form and gentlemanly bearing" had become so associated with the office of chief of police one could not think of the position without thinking of Heck. Heck insisted he was still a young man. Certainly no swain ever carried a more courtly bearing, agreed the editor.

The Lawton *Enterprise* backed Heck also, reporting that it was frequently heard on Lawton streets, "I'm willing to vote for Uncle Heck just as long as he wants the place."[26]

As the primary election neared, no person in Lawton seemed closer to the hearts of the people than Chief of Police Heck Thomas. But on that day, something went awry. Heck went down in defeat to fellow Democrat Robert McCalmant. In the general election, McCalmant was beaten by Republican Ed Gibson.

On May 6, Gibson was sworn in as the new chief of police.[27] Immediately, Heck pinned his prized gold badge onto Chief Gibson's shirt with the understanding that Gibson's friends would present him with a new badge of his own shortly.[28]

So, for the first time in Lawton's history, the city had a Republican chief of police. For the first time in Heck's thirty years as a law officer, he found himself without a job.

Chapter 15

Into the Sunset

Matie always believed Heck's game chickens helped defeat him in the election for city marshal in 1909. Some people had criticized him for participating in the activity. At school, the other children taunted Beth and Harley. "Yah-h-h-h, your old daddy got beat!" one boy told Beth. This made her so angry she could have spit in his face, but she didn't tell her father about the incident.

The rumor circulated that Heck had a federal deputy marshalship waiting for him, "to be tendered shortly."[1] Meantime, he was offered several other appointments, some reportedly "prominently connected with state administration." But desiring to remain in Lawton, Heck refused to consider anything which would take him from there.[2] In June, State Game Warden Askew of Chickasha approached Heck about a commission as state deputy game warden.[3] Though his health was still poor, Heck accepted the job, which took him back to riding outdoors.

That summer, Albert came for another visit, much to Heck's delight. Reverend Mowbray died, and Matie, Harley, and Beth rode the train to Tulsa for the funeral.

In January 1910, Heck's long-expected commission for U.S. deputy marshal came through. Marshal John Abernathy appointed him office deputy for the Western District of Oklahoma with headquarters in Lawton. Returning to the marshal's office, Heck found a lot had changed since he left the marshal service ten years ago. Things were quieter now, the criminal business, except for federal offenses, having been committed to state offices at statehood. The deputy marshal force was much smaller. Heck did most of his out-of-town traveling on the train or by auto now, instead of by horse.[4] While he had grown older and man hunting was easier these days, he had lost none of the determination of his younger days. When he went after a man, he found him or else the fugitive was not in the country.[5]

Sometimes when Heck rode out around Lawton in his horse and buggy to deliver a warrant or to summon a witness, he took Beth with him. Missing school didn't bother her that much, for admittedly, she "wasn't that much of a student." She loved going with her father and just being with him. Sometimes Heck sang to her, usually the old religious songs he had learned as a boy, but mostly they talked. This way, Beth was sure her father put a lot of things into her heart and mind that she would not have thought of otherwise; things like life in general and moral principals. Beth always felt safe and secure when her father was around.

But even then, the malady which had afflicted Heck so much during the past three years was troubling him again. Though suffering a lot of pain when on their trips together, he never talked to Beth about feeling bad.

Heck loved his family. Beth recalled one night when they were all sitting in the living room, Harley and Beth studying, Matie doing her "fancy work," and Heck reading. Heck laid down his newspaper and glanced around at the rest of them with a look of contentment. "To see my family all around me here, this is about as close to heaven as I ever expect to get," he said.

That summer, though feeling poorly, Heck made his last trip to Georgia to visit the rest of his family. By now, he had seven grandchildren, some of whom he had never seen before. Through the years, each of his children by his first marriage had brought their own children up on the heroic tales of their grandfather.[6] With pride, they recounted Heck's Civil War escapades, his fight with Sam Bass, the tracking of the Jim and Pink Lee gang, trailing the Dalton gang, and the killing of Bill Doolin. Because of the valor of their grandfather, Heck's grandchildren quickly became heroes in their neighborhoods. When Heck arrived, his grandchildren invited their friends to gather around the veteran office to hear more tales.[7] Heck returned home happy, aware this was probably his last visit back East.

In December 1910, U.S. Marshal John Abernathy of the Western District was accused of wrongdoing on false charges. Angry, he went to Washington and demanded to see the original charge, or a copy thereof.[8] He was told the paper had been mislaid. Learning of Abernathy's quandary, Heck wrote to Oklahoma's blind senator, Thomas Gore, urging him to talk to Abernathy before he resigned.[9] But Heck's letter did not reach Senator Thomas until too late. Abernathy had already quit in disgust at all the red tape and chicanery. Chief office deputy in Guthrie, Chris Madsen, assumed top command as temporary marshal. Madsen quickly renewed Heck's commission as office deputy in Lawton.

As usual when a new marshal took over, the newly selected deputy marshal force made the trip to Guthrie to settle up their accounts. Here, in the Federal Building, they would take the oath of allegiance anew if they were being retained, and

Though ill, Heck Thomas made a final trip back East to see his family one last time. Pictured above with his three sons from l: Lovick Thomas, Henry A. Thomas, Heck Thomas, and Albert M. Thomas. Courtesy Thomas Collection.

receive any special instructions that the incoming marshal had to give.

Bundled against the severe cold, Heck rode the train to Guthrie on New Year's Day, 1911. The half-dozen deputies there in the brightly lit office of the Federal Building that night were described by a reporter from the *Oklahoman* as the "survivors of the fittest."[10]

He noted that among them was Allen G. Goff, an Ohioan who had been a Texas ranger from 1877 to 1881 and had entered the Marshal's service in 1882 and had been there ever since. Heck was there too, still looking dapper in his Prince Albert coat, "a genial, likable, elderly gentleman." Present also was John Paul Jones, a Missourian whom Marshal Grimes had first commissioned in 1890; A. Jacobson, a Dane like Madsen, with ten years service; D.A. Haden, a Texan with five years service; and Marshal Madsen.

As usual when the deputy marshals got together, they couldn't help but talk about the past. Intrigued, the reporter listened as such names as Ned Christie, the Verdigris Kid, the Daltons, Bill Doolin, Cook gang, Casey gang, and Cherokee Bill ran through their stories. Jones heckled Heck about his old time nickname of Scissortail.

Violent death figured conspicuously in the narratives of the older deputies, mingled with stories of long rides through blizzards and snowstorms, of ambushes, and of unsuccessful pursuit and starvation.

Outside the Federal Building, the wind raged on one of the coldest nights Oklahoma had experienced that winter. Recalling past trips into such storms while man hunting, Madsen commented, "What a night this would be to start, eh!"

Heck burst into song: *"Ti-i, ki-i, yoop-ee, yoop-ee, yai-ai-ai!"* Then he threatened the news reporter with "everlasting damnation" if he printed that refrain from the old cowboy and frontier song.[11]

But at last, all the subpoenas were made out, and though it was a Sabbath and New Year's night, the government could not wait. The deputies, "who could for hours tell tales from their own experience that were stranger than fiction," bid Marshal Madsen goodbye. They drifted off to the various depots with a pocketful of subpoenas to be served in some mild civil business rather than in pursuit of some dangerous outlaw as they had done once.

Heck did not work long after that. In the spring of 1911, he suffered a violent attack from his kidney ailment and was forced to retire from the marshal's office.[12] From then on most of what little money he earned was spent on trying to regain his health.[13] He lost weight rapidly and was in and out of Lawton's new hospital. A few times when able to do so, he drove the buggy downtown. He walked unsteadily on the street, but still appeared jaunty and debonair, his one suit clean and pressed.[14]

Most of the time, Heck chose to stay around home. His game chickens gave him something to do. By then, Beth was twelve-years-old, large for her age. Once when Heck stood in the yard, he looked so frail, she picked him up to see if she could. He scolded her, "Honey, you'll hurt yourself."

Beth helped Heck take care of his chickens and horse and colt. Once Heck caught her riding the colt, which she had done before, unbeknown to him. But this time he had seen her and it scared him. He admonished, "Don't you ever do that again, honey; you'll get hurt."

But Beth loved the horses. One day she was riding Heck's saddle horse, and the mare ran away with her. It was her own fault, Beth admitted. She liked to ride fast. She egged the horse on a little too much. "Boy, she really put the miles on," Beth remembered. She hung onto the saddlehorn, until the horse stopped. Beth did not report this incident to her father.

Heck grew weaker and weaker. One bright, sunny day, he asked Harley to drive him to the country in the buggy so he could hunt some game. He tried to lift his gun and could not. He quietly asked Harley to take him home, and never went out again.

From July on, Heck lay bedfast. In those days, the government offered no type of retirement, disability, or medical payment. Neither did Heck have anything coming in the way of retirement from the Lawton Police Department nor Fire Department. John Lantznester and Heck's other Confederate friends in the A.P. Hill Camp V.C.V. tried to help him obtain a Civil War pension. But officials in Washington turned down his application. They said there was no proof that Heck had served in that war, and that he had been too young and had not been formally enlisted.

How Heck's family made it financially those days, Beth didn't know. "We were awfully poor," she said. Her grandparents had never been wealthy, but when Reverend Mowbray died, he left his wife well-fixed. "Grandmother probably helped Mother, as did Aunt Annie," Beth said. Once, Heck borrowed twenty-five dollars from Madsen.

Then there was the old, one-armed saloon-keeper by the name of Mike Markeson, who tried to run a decent place. After Heck got down and was so sick, Markeson looked after him as a son. Each day during the summertime, Markeson had the ice company leave ice for Heck so he could have a cold drink. Markeson helped Heck in many other ways and came to see him often. The saloon-keeper gave Beth her first ride in an automobile, a long remembered, exhilarating experience.

That last year of his life, Heck suffered in continuous pain. Still he never talked about feeling bad—at least not to Beth and Harley. "He was the most cheerful, uncomplaining person I ever saw," Beth said.

Heck had friends galore who came to see him, and to help him pass the time away. Once, after Emmett Dalton got out of prison, he came to see Heck. Dalton was trying to get a U.S. deputy marshal's job and wanted Heck to help him. Heck didn't want to do that. After Dalton left, he wrote a letter to S.G. Victor, U.S. Marshal of the Eastern District at Muskogee, protesting Dalton's application.

Victor replied: "I heartily agree with you that men who have led a criminal life and have always been an enemy of the law and those enforcing the law should not now be put in position to attempt to enforce the law."[15]

Dalton did not get the job.

On the point of financial desperation, Heck applied once more for a state deputy game warden commission during the fall of 1911. Democrat Lee Cruce was running for governor of Oklahoma. He promised Heck the job if he would help him get elected governor in November. Heck threw his support to Cruce and urged his friends to vote from him. Cruce won the election, but nothing more was said about Heck's commission. After that Heck seemed to give up.

At Christmas, some of the citizens of Lawton expressed their love for Heck with a generous offering. He thanked them in a public announcement. For the first time, some of his bitterness and desperation showed: [16]

THOMAS THANKS FRIENDS
I desire to thank my friends who manifested their kindness to me in such a substantial manner Xmas.

"You know I appreciate your kindness deeply, and that my being a physical wreck is by no carlessness [sic] of my own. About eight years ago I sustained a severe heart injury while running to a fire (I was chief of the volunteer fire company at the time) and it has grown worse from year to year until I am practically an invalid, but am anxious to go to work at anything I can make good at.

Many of my friends know that I am entitled to a pension from the federal government having been wounded twice in government service and that if such a law was in force, I am entitled to a pension from this city as with the help of other volunteers I have kept this town from burning many times in early days when we had little protection from fires and it was in an effort of this kind that I sustained the injury that causes my disability.

Respectfully, HECK THOMAS

Winter passed and the new year came in. Several times during that spring and summer of 1912, Heck was listed in critical condition. Twice his exceptional rallying power pulled him through. Following his third attack, Dr. Dunlap, his attending physician, sent him again to St. Anthony's Hospital in Oklahoma City. A number of his old friends from frontier days visited him there.

Said one: "It was a sad sight to see my old friend, who weighed 200 pounds in the old days, reduced too less than 150 and weak in proportion. When Oklahoma gets time and advances further there should be a system of insurance devised to touch cases of this kind. Heck informs me that he is out of work now, and that for several years, outside of a bare living, all that he has made has been spent in seeking health."[17]

On Heck's return from St. Anthony's, Dr. Dunlap offered his prognosis. "The illness is serious though not critical," he said. "Mr. Thomas has heart, kidney and liver trouble. His heart has been bothering him especially. If he recovers, he will never be in good health again."[18]

But Heck was not to see that day. His pain-racked body was not sufficiently strong enough to overcome this third attack. When he knew he was not going to make it, he said the biggest regret he had was that he wouldn't live to see Harley, fourteen, and Beth, thirteen, reared.

Too weak to write for himself, Heck dictated a final letter to Matie for Madsen:[19]

>
> Lawton, Okla.
> August 5, 1912
>
> Dear Chris,
>
> This malady is troubling me again, and I know I have not the strength or the inclination to resist it, so no matter what happens I do not want you or Tilghman to come over here, and no flowers. If I had got work, I would have paid you that $25.00.
>
> Give my love to Reno, the best boy in the country to whom I owe a letter. Remember me to Marion—the dear sweet little girl—and tell her she knows we always loved her. Tell them life is a constant burden and misery and I hope I will not be here long. Love to all and good-by forever.
>
> Your friend, Heck Thomas

Later, Madsen related to Matie that tears had coursed down his cheeks when he read the letter in his office at Guthrie. His hand shook as he laid the note down. He predicted in a quavery voice, "Poor old Heck, we may hear of his death at any moment."[20]

During Heck's last few days, he lay unconscious the greater portion of the time. At brief intervals he recognized his family and friends and greeted them cordially. Mrs. Mowbray, Annie Archer, and her son, James, arrived from Tulsa; Mrs. D.C. Graham, a niece of Heck's on his mother's side, came from Oklahoma City. Heck tried to sing a song with her: *"I wandered, today, to the hills, Maggie . . . "* but he couldn't.

By Tuesday, August 13, Heck lay in a coma.[21] The following day, those present thought he would not live through the evening. At two a.m. he was still breathing, but it was only a question of hours, however, possibly minutes, how much longer he could survive.[22]

Those final moments were burned vividly into Beth's memory. All of the family was at her father's bedside, along with Dr. Dunlap and John Lantznester, Heck's close friend. They took turns wiping the death sweat off Heck's brow. Beth went in and laid down across the foot of her bed while her father lingered. When they called her, she returned to the other room. Heck breathed his last at four a.m., and Matie fainted.

Then the strangest thing happened, according to Beth. Matie had a mantel clock that her father had given her one Christmas. Eventually, the clock got tired of running and quit. But the moment Heck died, the clock struck. Beth had heard of such things happening before, but she had never believed it before.

Now, as the full realization of her father's death swept over her, it broke her heart. She knew she had lost the dearest friend in the world to her.

Chapter 16

Aftermath

That Sunday, one of the longest funeral processions to ever assemble in Lawton gathered to follow Heck Thomas' body to the cemetery. Beforehand, everyone crowded the Presbyterian Church to attend the service. "They were not there through idle curiosity, but to honor the man they had known and loved."[1] True to Heck's wishes, neither Chris Madsen nor Bill Tilghman was present.

The pall bearers sat in a solemn row, Col. R.A. Sneed, C.G. Joy, J.M. Diffendaffer, John Lantznester, all Confederate veterans, next to Robert Stevens and Fire Chief Sim Sheppard. Someone sang "Abide With Me," then Rev. R.T. Irwin, who had been faithful in visiting Heck during his long illness, delivered the message. Heck was laid to rest in Lawton's Highland Cemetery in John Lantznester's lot. A public subscription paid his funeral expenses.[2]

Heck left no estate, small reward for one who had done so much to maintain law and order in the Southwest. Even his house was mortgaged and Matie realized nothing from its sale.

During those last long days of his illness, Heck and Matie had discussed what the family should do after he was gone. Together, they decided it would be best for Matie and the girls to move back to Tulsa to be near Matie's family. Following the funeral, Matie sold everything she could, gave away the dogs, and she and the girls left Lawton on the train one week after Heck's death. There, Matie opened a boarding house, and Harley and Beth immediately started to school and went to work parttime for the telephone company, in spite of their young ages.

Heck had seen many changes in the land since first coming to Indian Territory. He helped bring order out of chaos and made it possible for civilized conditions to exist on the frontier. Man hunting had changed from one lonely deputy riding his horse hard on the trail of an outlaw to sophisticated surveillance teams of men in automobiles. During battle, he had been wounded six times and seen eight men die at his side, an experience which always disturbed him deeply.

Once when Heck heard a gunman talk about dying with his boots on, he said, "Kid stuff. Nothing to be proud of, letting another man get the drop on you."[3]

Heck held a certain amount of admiration for the sportsmanship of the gunmen of territorial days.[4] He did not believe Doolin ever shot a victim in the back. He also knew Doolin did not make a practice of robbing needy individuals. Instead, he and his gang went after organized capital—the railroads, banks, and express companies. If Doolin took a horse or forced a lonely rancher to feed his men, it was because of dire necessity and he always tried to compensate that person.

In the early 1970s, Richard Boone, who appeared in the television series, "Hec Ramsey," which was reportedly based upon Heck's life, referred to Heck as "one of God's greatest iconoclasts . . . a former gunslinger turned lawman."[5] This infuriated Beth. An iconoclast, she said, is one who attacks established beliefs or institutions. Her father was anything but that. He believed in God. He stood for law and order and the rights of the average citizen. "He thought an officer of the law should be honest and above reproach at all times," she said.

Heck Thomas devoted his entire life to law and order. No finer gentleman ever accepted the hazardous tasks that he carried out so willingly and effectively.

"He did more to Christianize the Chickasaw and Choctaw Nations than all the ministers sent here," eulogized a Paul's Valley minister, following Heck's death.[6]

On May 15, 1969, the Oklahoma Sheriff and Peace Officers Association and the Oklahoma Highway Patrol unveiled a monument dedicated to Oklahoma law enforcement officers killed in the line of duty and to the Three Guardsmen. It is located in front of the Oklahoma Department of Public Safety at 36th Street and Martin Luther King Boulevard in Oklahoma City. The granite stone is etched with a likeness of The Three Guardsmen, "Oklahoma's U.S. Deputy Marshals." .

In 1988, the Smithsonian sponsored a traveling exhibit titled "America's Star: U.S. Marshals 1789-1989, using thirty mahogany cases to display more than three hundred artifacts illustrating the history and contemporary duties of the nation's oldest law enforcement agency. It opened in the Supreme Court in Washington, D.C., and moved on for a twenty-seven month run in twelve cities, the first of which was in the Cowboy Hall of Fame and Western Heritage Center in Oklahoma City.

Among those items on display were busts of the Three Guardsmen. These sculptures were done by Guthrie artist Fred Olds and appeared courtesy of the Oklahoma Territorial Museum. The exhibit's historian acclaimed the three deputies as the most famous of all the marshals who worked in Oklahoma and Indian Territories. He labeled the bust of Heck Thomas as the "Best of the Best."

Today, Heck's Colt revolver, his 44.40 Winchester, and his shotgun, which killed Bill Doolin, remain on permanent display in Lawton's Great Plains Museum. His gold badge, which he wore as Lawton's first city marshal, is there also. Because of her impoverished condition, in 1924 Matie had sold the badge for twenty-five dollars to Tulsa oilman Frank Billingslea, who in turn gave it to actor Randolph Scott. Scott proudly wore it in many western movies in which he appeared. He gave the badge to the museum in 1958 following a request by Heck's daughter, Beth Thomas Meeks. [7]

At one time, the story came out in a Lawton newspaper that Heck's gravesite had been lost. "Why didn't they ask me about," Beth spoke indignantly. "I've always known where he was buried." To avoid such a thing happening again, the Thomas family purchased a pink sandstone marker and erected it over Heck Thomas' grave.

Beth remained her father's staunchest supporter to the end of her life. She died in 1991 at the age of ninety-two.

ENDNOTES

Chapter 1
1. "Of the Death of General Kearney," Letter to the Editor, Atlanta *Constitution,*____ , Thomas Papers.
2. Fort Smith *Elevator,* Nov. 21, 1877.
3. *Ibid.,* Feb. 25, 1887.
4. Guthrie *Daily Capital,* Oct. 17, 1895.

Chapter 2
1. "Thomas Family History," handwritten manuscript, Thomas Papers.
2. *Ibid.*
3. C. Winn Upchurch, "The Real Heck Ramsey," Atlanta *Journal and Constitution Magazine,* Feb. 18, 1973.
4. *Ibid.*
5. James Callaway, "General Edward Lloyd Thomas,"undated clipping, Thomas Papers.
6. Letter, Colin S. Monteith, Jr. to Mrs. J. B. Meeks, Mar. 16, 1970, Thomas Papers.
7. James Callaway, "General Edward Lloyd Thomas," undated clipping, Thomas Papers.
8. *Ibid.*
9. L.P. Thomas, Sr. the 2nd, "Thomas Family History," Atlanta, Nov. 15, 1900, Thomas Papers.
10. "Battle of Atlanta," Atlanta *Constitution,* undated clipping, Thomas Papers.
11. "Thomas Family History," *op. cit.*
12. "Bruff's Column," Atlanta *Constitution,* undated clipping, Thomas Papers.
13. *Ibid.*
14. *Ibid.*
15. *Ibid.*
16. *Ibid.*

Chapter 3

1. Letter, Franklin M. Garrett, Atlanta Historical Society, Sept. 5, 1979.
2. Frank Daniel, "Atlanta's Bleakest Christmas," *Atlanta Journal-Constitution Magazine,* Dec. 20, 1964.
3. "Bruff's Column," Atlanta *Constitution,* undated clipping, Thomas Papers.
4. Daniel, *op. cit.*
5. *Ibid.*
6. Glenn Shirley, *Heck Thomas: Frontier Marshal* (Philadelphia, New York: Chilton Co. Book Division, 1962, p. _.)
7. Matie Mowbray Thomas, "Outlaws," Grant Foreman Indian Pioneer History, Vol. 90, pp. 132-137.
8. "Bruff's Column," Atlanta *Constitution,* undated clipping, Thomas Papers.
9. *Ibid.*
10. *Ibid.*
11. *Ibid.*
12. *Ibid.*
13. Undated clipping, Thomas Papers.

Chapter 4

1. "Heck Thomas," handwritten manuscript, Thomas Papers.
2. Statement of Recommendation for Henry A. Thomas, from Atlanta Citizens, Atlanta, Georgia, Apr. 8, 1876, Thomas Papers
3. Letter, Franklin M. Garrett, Atlanta Historical Society, Sept. 5, 1979.
4. Galveston *Daily News,* Feb. 24, 1878.
5. *Ibid.*
6. "Heck Thomas," *op. cit.*
7. Galveston *Daily News,* Mar. 20, 1878.
8. Walter Prescott Webb, *The Texas Rangers* (New York: Houghton Mifflin Company, 1935, pp. 371-391).
9. "Heck Thomas," *op. cit.*
10. *Ibid.*

11. Galveston *Daily News*, Apr. 9, 1878.
12. Walter Prescott Webb, *The Texas Rangers* (New York: Houghton Mifflin Company, 1935, pp. 371-391).
13. *Ibid.*
14. Matie Mowbray Thomas, "Outlaws," Grant Foreman Indian Pioneer History, Vol. 90, pp. 132-137.
15. Galveston *Daily News*, Feb. 24, 1885.
16. *Ibid*, Mar. 5, 1885.
17. *Ibid*, Apr. 8, 1885.
18. Zoe A. Tilghman, "How Heck Hexed the Outlaws," *Orbit Magazine*, Jan. 3, 1960.
19. *The Daily Oklahoman*, Nov. 10, 1935.
20. Thomas, "Outlaws," *op. cit.*, p. 111.
21. The Galveston *Daily News*, Sept. 10, 1885.
22. Thomas, "Outlaws," *op. cit.*, p. 111.
23. Undated clipping, Thomas Papers.
24. Galveston *Daily News*, Sept.. 10, 1885.

Chapter 5

1. *The Daily Oklahoman*, Feb. 10, 1957.
2. *Ibid.*
3. Fort Smith *Elevator*, January 8, 1886.
4. *Ibid.*
5. *Ibid.*
6. *Ibid.*, May 26, 1886.
7. *The Daily Oklahoman*, Feb. 10, 1957.
8. *Ibid.*
9. Fort Smith *Elevator*, Jan. 8, 1886.
10. *Ibid.*, Jan. 7, 1886.
11. *Ibid.*, Jan. 5, 1885.
12. *Ibid.*, Jan. 2, 1885.
13. *Ibid.*
14. *Ibid.*, Jan. 26, 1887.
15. *Ibid.*, Dec. 2, 1887.
16. Glenn Shirley, *Heck Thomas: Frontier Marshal* (Phila-

delphia-New York, Chilton Co. Book Division, p. 82).
17. Fort Smith *Elevator*, July 29, 1887.
18. Vinita (I.T.) *Republican,* undated clipping, Thomas Papers.
19. Fort Smith *Elevator,* Dec. 9, 1887.
20. *Ibid,* Apr. 22, 1886.
21. Chickasaw (Indian Territory) *Enterprise,* Jan. 15, 1887.
22. *Ibid.*
23. "An Atlanta Man Going to the Klondike," undated clipping, Thomas Papers.
24. Fort Smith *Elevator,* Aug. 10, 1888.
25. *Ibid.,* Sept. 28, 1888.
26. Matie Mowbray Thomas, "Outlaws,"Grant Foreman Indian-Pioneer History, Vol. 90, pp. 132-136.
27. Undated clipping, Thomas Papers.
28. William P. Steven, "Walter Ferguson's Last 'News Tip' Brings Story of Early Outlaw Days," Tulsa *Tribune,* Mar. 15, 1936.

Chapter 6

1. Matie Mowbray Thomas, "Early Life of the Methodist Church In Tulsa," Grant Foreman Indian Pioneer History, Vol. 90, pp. 120-131.
2. Matie Mowbray Thomas, "Mowbray Family History," handwritten manuscript, Thomas Papers.
3. Matie Mowbray Thomas, "Our Trip to Tulsa in 1888," handwritten manuscript, Thomas Papers.
4. Angie Debo, *Tulsa* (Norman: University of Oklahoma Press, 1943, p. 55).
5. Mowbray, "Our Trip to Tulsa in 1888," *op. cit.*
6. Matie Mowbray Thomas, "Early Life of the Methodist Church In Tulsa," op. cit., pp. 142-148.
7. *Ibid.*
8. Angie Debo, *Tulsa* (Norman: University of Oklahoma Press, 1943, p. 55).
9. Matie Mowbray Thomas, "Outlaws," Grant Foreman Indian-Pioneer History, Vol. 90, pp. 132-136

10. *Ibid.*
11. Letter, Colin Monteith, Jr. to Mrs. J.B. Meeks, Apr. 26, 1961, Thomas Papers.
12. William P. Steven, "Walter Ferguson's Last 'News Tip' Brings Story of Early Outlaw Days," Tulsa *Tribune*, Mar. 15, 1936.
13. Matie Mowbray Thomas, "Early Day Weddings In Indian Territory in Tulsa," Grant Foreman Indian Pioneer History, Vol. 90, p. 128.

Chapter 7

1. Tombstone, Ned Christie. Also see Phillip Steele, *The Last Cherokee Warriors*, Pelican Publishing Company, Gretna, Louisiana, 1974, p. 72.
2. Common Law Record, Vol. 30 RG 21, 1886 to Aug. 17, 1887, U.S. Court, Western District of Arkansas, Federal Archives and Records Center, Fort Worth, Texas.
3. Fort Smith Elevator, May 31, 1889.
4. *Ibid.*, Oct.3,1889.
5. Heck Thomas Day Book, 1889-90, p. 30, Thomas Papers.
6. Muskogee *Phoenix*, Oct. 3, 1889.
7. *Ibid.*
8. Fort Smith *Elevator*, Oct. 3, 1889.
9. Muskogee *Phoenix*, Oct. 3, 1889.
10. Fort Smith *Elevator*, Oct. 11, 1889.
11. Heck Thomas Day Book, 1889-90, p. 32, Thomas Papers.
12. Steele, *op. cit.*, p. 91.
13. Heck Thomas Day Book, 1889-90, p. 41, Thomas Papers.

Chapter 8

1. "Country Boy," *Daily Oklahoman*, Feb. 2, 1960.
2. "Little Stories of Men Whose Lives Overflow with Danger," (Special to *Daily Oklahoman)*, Jan. 7, 1911.
3. Fort Smith, *Elevator*, Dec. 2, 1887.
4. *Ibid.*, Sept. 12, 1890.
5. *Ibid.*

6. *Daily Oklahoma State Capital,* May 24, 1893.
7. Undated clipping, Thomas Papers.
8. "Hunting the Daltons," undated clipping, Thomas Papers
9. "Must Be Real Detectives," undated clipping, Thoma. Papers.
10. The Tulsa *Democrat,* August 18, 1918.
11. *Ibid.*
12. "Thomas' Reward," Guthrie *Oklahoma State Capital,* undated clipping, Thomas Papers.
13. *Ibid.*
14. *Ibid.*
15. Evett Dumas Nix, *Oklahombres* (St. Louis: Copyright E.D. Nix, 1929, p. 104).
16. Croy, *op. cit.*
17. Evett Dumas Nix, *Oklahombres* (St. Louis: Copyright E. D. Nix, 1929, p. 104).
18. Undated clipping, Thomas Papers.
19. Guthrie *Daily Leader,* Feb. 25, 1895.
20. *Ibid.*
21. Albert Thomas to Mrs. Beth Meeks, Aug. 28, 1958, Thomas Papers.
22. Guthrie *Daily Leader, July* 29, 1894.
23. *Ibid.*, Sept. 8, 1895.

Chapter 9

1. "Thomas Receives a Role," undated clipping, Thomas Papers.
2. *Ibid.*
3. Glenn Shirley, *Heck Thomas: Frontier Marshal* (Philadelphia-New York, Chilton Co. Book Division, 1962, p. 204).
4. William P. Steven, "Walter Ferguson's Last 'News Tip' Brings Store of Early Outlaw Days," Tulsa *Tribune,* Mar.15, 1936.
5. Fort Smith *Times-Democrat* (Guthrie, Aug. 25, 1896).
6. William N. Randolph, "Heck Thomas, Oklahoma Officer Unafraid," undated clipping, Thomas Papers.

7. Steven, op. cit.
8. Matie Mowbray Thomas, "Outlaws," Grant Foreman Indian Pioneer History, Vol. 90, pp. 132-136.
9. *Ibid.*
10. Letter, Bill Tilghman to Mrs. Matie Thomas, Oct. 7, 1920, Thomas Papers.
11. Shirley, *op. cit.*
12. *Ibid.*
13. Undated clipping, Thomas Papers.
14. *Ibid.*
15. "Heroes of Oklahoma," undated clipping, Thomas Papers.

Chapter 10

1. Initiated and Assembled by Lawton-Business and Professional Woman's Club, *'Neath August Sun* (Lawton: 1951, p. 6).
2. Undated clipping, Thomas Papers.
3. *'Neath August Sun, op. cit.*
4. El Reno *American News,* Aug. 1, 1901.
5. *Ibid.*
6. *'Neath August Sun, op. cit.* p. 14.
7. El Reno *American News,* Aug. 1, 1901.
8. *'Neath August Sun, op. cit.*, p. 148
9. *Ibid.*, p. 6.
10. *Ibid.*, p. 163.
11. Lawton *Daily Democrat,* Aug. 6, 1901.
12. *'Neath August Sun, op. cit.*, p. 185.
3. *Ibid.*, p. 158.
14. *Ibid.*, p.185.
15. Morris Swett, "Henry Andrews (sic) Thomas," *Chronicles of Comanche County,* Vol. VII, No 1, Spring 1961, pp. 31-49.
16. *'Neath August Sun, op. cit.* p. 144.
17. Lawton *Constitution,* Mar. 10, 1944.
18. Harley Joiner, phone interview, Sept. 15, 1979.
19. Morris Swett, "Henry Andrews (sic) Thomas," *Chronicles of Comanche County,* Vol. VII, No. 1, Spring 1961, pp. 31.

20. *Ibid.*, pp. 31-49.
21. *Ibid.*
22. Senator T.P. Gore, letter to Heck Thomas, Lawton, Oklahoma, Dec. 21, 1910.
23. Lawton *Constitution,* Mar. 10, 1944.

Chapter 11

1. Initiated and Assembled by Lawton Business and Professional Woman's Club, *'Neath August Sun* (Lawton: 1951, p. 99).
2. Morris Swett, "The Big Fire," *Chronicles of Comanche County,* Vol. 3, Spring 1957, p. 15.
3. *'Neath August Sun, op. cit.* p. 48.
4. Lawton *News,* Feb.5, 1902.
5. Undated clipping, Thomas Papers.
6. Lawton *Constitution,* Feb. 3, 1902.
7. Lawton *News,* Mar. 6, 1902.
8. *'Neath August Sun, op. cit.*, p. 194.
9. *Ibid.*, p. 193.
10. Undated clipping, Thomas Papers, Apr. 21, 1902.
11. Undated clipping, Thomas Papers, May 31, 1902.
12. *Oklahoma Principle Cities,* (__, p. 159).
13. Lawton *News,* Nov. 7, 1902.
14. "Revenue of Police Court," undated clipping, Thomas Papers.
15. *Ibid.*
16. *'Neath August Sun, op. cit.*, p.__).
17. "Fireman's Ball a Success," undated clipping, Thomas Papers.
18. "Dinner for Their Friends," undated clipping, Thomas Papers.
19. Swett, *op. cit.*
20. *'Neath August Sun, op. cit.*, p. 86.
21. *Ibid.*, p. 4.

Chapter 12

1. Initiated and Assembled by Lawton Business and Profes-

sional Woman's Club, *Neath August Sun* (Lawton: 1951, p. 86), p. 194.
   2. *Ibid.*, p. 144.
   3. Lawton *Constitution,* May 12, 1904.
   4. "From Tuesday Daily News," Apr. 14, 1904, clipping, Thomas Papers.
   5. Lawton *Constitution,* May 12, 1904.
   6. *Ibid.*
   7. *Ibid.*
   8. "From Monday Daily News," Apr. 19, 1904, clipping, Thomas Papers.
   9. Lawton *News Republican*, Dec. 22, 1904.
   10. Lawton *Constitution,* Apr. 10, 1904.
   11. Lawton *News Republican,* Apr. 7, 1904.
   12. *Ibid.*
   13. *Ibid.*
   14. Lawton *News Republican,* Apr. 7, 1904.
   15. Lawton *Constitution,* May 12, 1904.
   16. "From Tuesday Daily News," Apr. 14, 1904.
   17. *Ibid.*

Chapter 13

   1. New York *Times,* Apr. 12, 1904.
   2. January_, 1906, clipping, Thomas Papers.
   3. Undated clipping, Thomas Papers.
   4. Undated clipping, Thomas Papers.
   5. "Daring Man Hunters," undated clipping, Thomas Papers.
   6. Initiated and Assembled by Lawton Business and Professional Woman's Club, *'Neath August Sun* (Lawton: 1951, p. 188).
   7. Lawton *News Republican,* Apr. 5, 1905.
   8. *Ibid.*, Nov. 29, 1906.

Chapter 14

   1. Lawton *News Republican,* Sept. 14, 1905.
   2. *Ibid.*, Sept. 30, 1905.

3. Lawton *Weekly State Democrat,* Oct. 19, 1905.
4. Lawton *News Republican,* Dec. 14, 1905.
5. *Ibid.*
6. *Ibid.,* Dec. 21, 1906.
7. *Ibid.,* Jan. 6, 1906.
8. *Ibid.,* June 21, 1906.
9. *Ibid.*
10. *Ibid.,* Nov. 29, 1906.
11. *Ibid.,* Dec. 26, 1906.
12. Undated clipping, Thomas Papers.
13. Lawton *Constitution,* Apr. 4, 1907.
14. "Marshal Thomas Receives a Beautiful Medal From a Concourse of Friends," undated clipping, Thomas Papers.
15. *Ibid.*
16. "Police Record," undated clipping, Thomas Papers.
17. Lawton *Constitution,* Nov. 6, 1907.
18. "Veteran Confederates Will Attend Inaugural Ceremonies," Lawton *Constitution,* Nov. 15, 1907.
19. "Sham Bank Robbery," undated clipping, Thomas Papers.
20. Zoe A. Tilghman, *Marshal of the Last Frontier,* (Glendale: Arthur H. Clark Co., 1964, p. 313).
21. *Ibid.,* p. 315.
22. William P. Steven, "Walter Ferguson's Last 'News Tip' Brings Story of Early Outlaw Days," Tulsa *Tribune,* Mar. 15, 1936.
23 *Ibid.*
24. Undated clipping, Thomas Papers.
25. "Heck Thomas Puts Out His Platform," Lawton *Constitution,* Apr. 3, 1909.
26. Lawton *Enterprise,* undated clipping, Thomas Papers.
27. April_, 1909, clipping, Thomas Papers.
28. *Ibid.*

Chapter 15

1. "But Few Changes After All," undated clipping, Thomas Papers.

2. *Ibid.*
3. Lexington *Leader,* June 24, 1909.
4. Matie Mowbray Thomas, "Outlaws," Grant Foreman Indian Pioneer History, Vol. 90, pp. 132-136.
5. "Indian Fighter Here," undated clipping, Thomas Papers.
6. Mrs. J.R. Smith, letter to Mrs. J.B. Meeks, May 5, 1973, Thomas Papers.
7. Collin S. Monteith, Jr., letter to Mrs. J.B. Meeks, Oct. 17, 1958, Thomas Papers.
8. Lawton *Constitution,* Dec. 29, 1910.
9. Senator T.P. Gore, letter to Heck Thomas, Lawton, Okla., Dec. 21, 1910, Thomas Papers.
10. *Oklahoman,* January 1, 1911.
11. *Ibid.*
12. Thomas, *op. cit.*
13. "Heck Thomas Goes Home to Lawton," *Oklahoman,* undated clipping, Thomas Papers.
14. Homer Croy, *Trigger Marshal: The Story of Chris Madsen* (Philadelphia-New York: Duell Sloan and Pearce, 1958, p. 235.
15. S.G. Victor, letter to Heck Thomas, Jan. 26, 1912, Thomas Papers.
16. "Thomas Thanks Friends," undated clipping, Thomas Papers.
17. "Heck Thomas Goes Home to Lawton," *op. cit.*
18. "Heck Thomas Is Very Ill," undated clipping, Thomas Papers.
19. Croy, *op. cit.*
20. "Heck Thomas Requests Old Friend To 'Send No Flowers,'" Lawton *Daily News and Star,* Aug. 11, 1912.
21. Lawton *Constitution,* Aug. 15, 1912.
22. "Death Expected Momentarily," undated clipping, Thomas Papers.

Chapter 16

1. "Throngs Follow Thomas Body to City Cemetery," undated clipping, Thomas Papers.

2. Lawton *Constitution,* Aug. 18, 1912.

3. Morris Swett, "Henry Andrews (sic) Thomas, *Chronicles of Comanche County, Vol.* VIII, No. 1, Spring 1961, pp. 31-49.

4. *Ibid.*

5. Winn C. Upchurch, "Heck Thomas, Gentleman Lawman," *Orbit Magazine,* Apr. 15, 1973.

6. Matie Mowbray Thomas, "Outlaws," Grant Foreman Indian Pioneer History, Vol. 90, pp. 132-136.

7. Oklahoma City *Times,* Nov. 30, 1960.

BIBLIOGRAPHY

A. BOOKS

Croy, Homer, *Trigger Marshal: The Story of Chris Madsen*, Philadelphia-New York: Duell Sloan and Pearce, 1958.

Debo, Angie, *Tulsa*, Norman: University of Oklahoma Press, 1943.

History of Oklahoma. Chickasha: __, 1924.

Horan, James D., *The Outlaws: The Authentic Wild West*, New York: Crown Publishing Company, 1977.

Hunter and Rose, *The Album of Gunfighters*.

'*Neath August Sun*, Lawton: Initiated and Assembled by Lawton Business and Professional Woman's Clubs, 1951.

Nix, Evett Dumas, *Oklahombres*. Copyright, E.D. Nix, St. Louis, 1929.

Oklahoma Principle Cities, __, __.

The Pioneer Citizens' Society of Atlanta, Pioneer Citizens' *History of Atlanta 1833-1902*. Atlanta: Byrd Printing Company, 1902.

Shirley, Glenn, *Heck Thomas: Frontier Marshal*. Philadelphia-New York: Chilton Company Book Division, 1962.

Shirley, Glenn, *The Law West of Fort Smith*. New York: Henry Holt and Company, 1957.

Shirley, Glenn, *Six Gun and Silver Star*, Albuquerque: University of New Mexico Press, 1955.

Tilghman, Zoe A., *Marshal of the Last Frontier*. Glendale, Calif.: The Arthur H. Clark Company, 1964.

Webb, Walter Prescott, *The Texas Rangers*. New York: Houghton Mifflin Company, 1935.

B. PERIODICALS

Chronicles of Comanche County, Vol. 3, Spring, 1957, "The Big Fire," by Morris Swett, p. 15+.

Chronicles of Comanche County, Vol. vii, No. 1, Spring 1961, "Henry Andrews [sic] Thomas," by Morris Swett, pp. 31-49.

Tulsa School Review, Vol. XIII, No. 6, Tulsa, OK, Feb. 1957.

C. PUBLICATIONS OF THE GOVERNMENT

Pamphlet: "Fort Smith," Government Printing Office, 1972, No. 515-966/26.

D. PRIMARY SOURCES
1. Collected Documents

Atlanta City Directory, 1867; 1870.
Galveston City Directory, 1875-1876, 1876-1877, 1878-1879.
Lawton City Directory, 1911, 1902.
Thomas Family History, Thomas Papers.
Mowbray Family History, Thomas Papers.
History, Fire Department, City of Lawton, 1979.

2. Letters

Brice, Donaly E., Texas State Archives, Sept. 19, 1979.
Cammack, Elaine, Office of the Registrar, University of Georgia, Sept. 11, 1979.
Corwin, Hugh, Lawton, Okla., Aug. 6, 1979.
Estes, David E., Special Collections, Emory University, Atlanta, Ga., Aug. 28, 1979.
Garrett, Franklin M., Historian, Atlanta Historical Society, Atlanta, Ga., Sept. 5, 1979.
Doolin, Edith, Ingalls, O.T., to Bill Doolin, June 25, 1896.
Gore, Senator T. P., Washington D. C., to the Hon. Heck Thomas, Lawton, Okla., Dec. 21, 1910.
Kelly, Ruth E., The Rosenburg Library, Galveston, Sept. 11, 1979; Sept. 22, 1979.
Kolstrom, Yvette M., Lawton Public Library, Lawton, Okla., Aug. 22, 1979; Sept. 25, 1979.
Langley, W.Y., U.S. Marshal, Adair, I.T. to Heck Thomas, Guthrie, Okla. Territory, Oct. 10, 1896.
Lanier, R.S., Macon, Ga., to L.P. Thomas, Oct. 25, 1885.
C. Madsen, Guthrie, Okla., to Matie Thomas, Jan. 27, 1937; Dec. 27, 1938.
Madsen, Reno, Fort Worth, Tx., to Beth Meeks, Aug. 18, 1958.
Monteith, Colin S., Jr., Columbia, S.C., to Mrs. J.B. Meeks, Oct. 17, 1958; Apr. 26, 1961; May 15, 1961; May 18, 1961; Sept. 10, 1968; Mar. 16, 1970.
Monteith, Colin S., Jr., Columbia, S.C., to Mrs. Myrtle Gibbs, City Clerk, Kiowa, Okla., Sept. 17, 1968.
Monteith, Colin S., Jr., Columbia, S.C., to Clinton A. McGlamery, Dallas, Tx., Sept. 17, 1968.
Parker, I.C., Fort Smith, Ark., to Grover Cleveland, President of the United States, Feb. 21, 1893.

Powell, J.D., Sheriff, Southwest City, Mo., to Heck Thomas, Guthrie, O.T., Mar. 17, 1897.
Scott, Randolph, to Mrs. J.B. Meeks, Nov. 14, 1960.
Smith, Mrs. J.R., Tampa, Florida, to Mrs. J.B. Meeks, May 5, 1973.
Thomas, Albert, Anaheim, California, to Matie Thomas, July 26,   .
Thomas, Albert, Anaheim, California, to Beth Meeks, Nov. 10, __; May 15, 1957; (undated); Jan. 25, 1958; Apr. 6, 1958; May 25,   1958; Aug. 28, 1958; Aug. 2, 1959.
Thomas, Hazel, Anaheim, California, to Beth Meeks, Jan. 26, 1960.
Thomas, Lovick H., Hialeah, Florida, to Beth Meeks, Mar. 27, 1973.
Thomas, Virginia, Hialeah, Florida, to Beth Meeks, Oct. 19, 1973.
Thomas, Wesley, W., Newman, Ga., to Lovick P. Thomas, Atlanta, Ga., Oct. 18, 1900.
Tilghman, Bill, Oklahoma City, Okla., to Mrs. Matie Thomas, Oct. 7, 1920.
Tilghman, Zoe A., Oklahoma City, Okla., to Mrs. J.B. Meeks, Feb. 22, 1957.
Tong, Marvin E., Director, Great Plains Historical Association, Lawton, Okla., to Mrs. J.B. Meeks, May 26, 1967; Oct. 10, 1960; Nov. 22, 1960; Dec. 9, 1960.
Upchurch, C. Winn, St. Petersburg, Florida, to Mrs. J.B. Meeks, Mar. 23, 1973.
Victor, S.G., United States Marshal's Office, Muskogee, Okla., Jan. 26, 1912, to Mr. Heck Thomas.
Wailes, Levin, Hazelwood, Miss., to Rev. Edward Lloyd Thomas, May 24, 1842.
Waner, Esther, Territorial Museum, Guthrie, Okla., Aug. 8, 1979.
Wiley, Bell I., Professor Emeritus of History, Emory University, Atlanta, Ga., Aug. 24, 1979.

3. Interviews

Joiner, Harley Thomas Crist, phone, Sept. 15, 1979.
Meeks, Beth Thomas, Feb. 28, 1979; Apr. 16, 1979; May 23, 1979; June 20, 1979.

E. UNPUBLISHED MATERIALS

Thomas, Heck, handwritten narrative, untitled, undated, Jim and Pink Lee gang; Doolin gang, Thomas Papers.
Thomas, Matie, handwritten narrative, "Our Trip to Tulsa in 1888," Thomas Papers.

Thomas, Matie, handwritten narrative, untitled, undated, history of Heck Thomas, Thomas Papers.

Thomas, Matie, handwritten narrative, untitled, undated, history of the death of Ed Davis and capture of murderer by Heck Thomas, Thomas Papers.

Thomas, Matie, Mowbray family history, Thomas Papers.

Thomas, A. (Albert) M., Thomas Family History, Sept. 26, 1911, Thomas Papers.

Thomas, L. P. Thomas, Sr. the 2nd, Thomas Family History, Atlanta, Ga., Nov. 15, 1900.

Thomas Family History, author unknown, Thomas Papers.

F. COLLECTIONS

Grant Foreman Indian Pioneer History, Vol. 90, pp. 155-164, Matie Mowbray Thomas, "A Quiet Christmas In Indian Territory, in 1887," Apr. 21, 1937.

Grant Foreman Indian Pioneer History, Vol. 90, pp. 128-131, Matie Mowbray Thomas, "Early Day Weddings In Indian Territory At Tulsa," Apr. 12, 1937, pp. 142-148, Matie Mowbray Thomas, "Early Life of the Methodist Church," 1937; pp. 120-126, Matie Mowbray Thomas, "History of the Methodist Episcopal Church," Apr. 16, 1937; pp. 132-137, Matie Mowbray Thomas, "Outlaws," Apr. 16, 1937.

Thomas Papers, Mrs. Beth Meeks, containing miscellaneous papers, documents, receipts, U S. Deputy Marshal Commissions for Heck Thomas, day books of Heck Thomas, Thomas Family Tree, Bill of Sale, C.E. Scofield, Guthrie, Okla. Territory, Jan. 7, 1896, to Heck Thomas, (horse stolen by Bill Doolin, led by him at time of death), Endorsement, Heck Thomas for U.S. Marshal, Cloud Chief, O.T., to Pres. Grover Cleveland; other papers.

Tilghman, William, University of Oklahoma, Phillips Collection, various papers.

G. OTHER SOURCES

Headstone Inscriptions, Atlanta Historical Society, Thomas Lovick Pierce, Jane Peeples Thomas, Mrs. Martha Thomas, Martha Fullwood Thomas, Lovick P. Thomas, Sr., Callie C. Thomas.

Obituary, Abstract, Col. Lovick Pierce Thomas, Jr., The Atlanta *Journal*, Atlanta Historical Society.

Chickasaw (I.T.) *Enterprise*, Jan. 15, 1887.

The Daily Oklahoman (Oklahoma City), May 31, 1968, Jan. 23, 1966, __ 1972, Sept. 15, 1968, Feb. 10, 1957.
Daily Oklahoma State Capital (Guthrie), May 25, 1883, to June 10, 1893.
El Reno (Okla.) *News*, Nov. 12, 1897.
Fort Worth (Tx.) *Press Sun*, July 23, 1961.
Fort Smith (Ark.) *Elevator*, Oct. 3, 1884, to Feb. 27, 1891.
The Galveston (Tx.) *Daily News*, Jan. 5, 1873 to Jan. 19, 1873; Jan. 1, 1878, to Mar. 20, 1878; Feb. 24, 1885, to Sept. 10, 1885.
Guthrie (O.T.) *Daily Capital*, Oct. 17, 1895.
Guthrie (Okla.) *Daily Capital*, Sept. 8, 1955, Oct. 17, 1895.
The Guthrie (O.T.) *Daily Leader*, Aug. 24, 1894; Feb. 25, 1894; July 29, 1894.
The Guthrie (Okla.) *Daily Leader*, Aug. 16, 1912; Jan. 10, 1969.
Oklahoma State Capital (Guthrie, O.T.), Nov. 17, 1892.
Lawton (Okla.) *Constitution*, Aug. 5, 1912; Apr. 25, 1902, to June 8, 1915; Jan. 25, 1906; Nov. 17, 1911; June 8, 1915; June 21, 1906, to Apr. 4, 1907.
The Lawton (Okla.) *Constitution-Democrat*, Jan. 7, 1909, to Aug. 17, 1912.
The Lawton (Okla.) *Constitution Morning Press*, Apr. 9, 1961.
The Lawton (Okla.) *Daily News and Star*, Nov. 6, 1907, to Nov. 17, 1907; Aug. 11, 1912, to Aug. 17, 1912.
The Lawton (Okla.) *News*, Aug. 28, 1902, to Nov. 7, 1902.
The Lawton (O.T.) *Daily Republican*, Jan. 12, 1902, to July 17, 1902.
The Lawton (O.T.) *News Republican*, Oct. 29, 1903; Apr. 14, 1904, to Dec. 26, 1906.
The Lawton (O.T.) *Republican*, July 27, 1901, to Sept. 28, 1905.
The Lawton (O.T.) *Weekly State Democrat*, October 19, 1905, to Feb. 8, 1906.
The Lexington (O.T.) *Leader*, June 25, 1909.
The New York Times, Nov. 20, 1905; Jan. 2, 1906; Apr. 12, 1905; Apr. 13, 1905.
The Oklahoma City (Okla.) *Times*, Nov. 30, 1950.
The Purcell (Okla.*) Register*, Oct. 30, 1958.
Stillwater (O.T.) *Gazette, Nov. 12, 1897.*
Tulsa (Okla.) *Daily World*, Jan. 11, 1959; Aug. 11, 1912.

I. CLIPPINGS

1. <u>Identified</u>

"Actor Presents Gold Star," Lawton *Constitution*, Nov. 1960.

"Bandits Glad When Heck Thomas Dies," Lawton *Globe-Democrat*, Aug. 25, 1912.

Burchardt, Bill, "The Greatest of the West's U.S. Marshals," Bill Burchardt, *Oklahoma's Orbit Magazine*, Nov. 16, 1958.

"Chum in Limelight, Chief Is Displeased," Lawton *Globe-Democrat*, (Special Dispatch, Oklahoma City), July 29, 1911.

"Condition Is Unchanged," Lawton, Aug. 1912.

"Country Boy," *Daily Oklahoman*, Feb. 2, 1960.

Daniel, Frank, "Atlanta's Bleakest Christmas," *The Atlanta Journal and Constitution Magazine*, Dec. 20, 1964.

"Death Expected Momentarily," Lawton Aug. 1912.

"Death 'With Boots On' Was As 'Bill' Wished," Tulsa (Okla.) *Daily World*, Nov. 1, 1924.

"Dead Guardsman Played Important Role In Quelling Texas and Oklahoma Desperadoes," Lawton (Okla.) *Constitution*, Aug. 22, 1912.

Douglas, Col. Clarence B., "Heck Thomas Collects," *The Daily Oklahoman*, Nov. 10, 1935.

"Early Marshals," El Reno *Daily Tribune*, Apr. 14, 1941.

"EXTRA" (fire), Lawton *News*, Mar. 6, 1902.

"Former Frontier Officer Dying," (Special, dateline Lawton), Aug. 10, 1912).

"Gun Fighter's Badge Is Given," *Oklahoma City Times*, Nov. 30, 1960.

"Heck Thomas Dies At Home In Lawton," (Special to the *News*,) Aug. 15, 1912.

"Heck Thomas Is Dead At Lawton," Guthrie (Special) Aug. 15, 1912.

"Heck Thomas Fought Outlaws," (Special Correspondence of the *Globe-Democrat*), Aug. 15, 1912.

"Heck Thomas Puts Out His Platform," Lawton *Constitution*, Apr. 3, 1909.

"How Bill Doolin Died," Ft. Smith *Times-Democrat* (dateline Guthrie, O.T., Aug. 25, 1896).

"How Heck Hexed the Outlaws," Zoe A. Tilghman, *Oklahoma Orbit*, Jan. 3, 1960, p. 6.

"Lawton Name of New Town," *Oklahoma Capital*, June 28, 1901.

"Lawton Mushrooms Overnight," *El Reno American News*, Aug. 1, 1901.

Libke, Aileen Stroud, "The Man Who Killed Ned Christie," *Oklahoma's Orbit Magazine*, Feb. 27, 1977.

"'Little School Teacher' Still Recalls Early Wild West Days," Tulsa *Tribune*, Feb. 2, 1950.

"Little Stories of Men Whose Lives Overflow With Danger," Guthrie (Special to *Daily Oklahoman*), Jan. 7, 1911.

Pebbles, Lynn, "Grave of Famed City Outlaw Killer Found," Lawton *Constitution Morning Press*, Dec. 1, 1957.

"Man Who Aided In Making Oklahoma Safe Place Dead," Guthrie (Okla.) *Post-Dispatch*, Aug. 24, 1912.

McKennon, C. H., "The Last Raid of the Dalton Gang," Tulsa *Sunday World*, July 7, 1974.

"More Gambling," Lawton (O.T.) *Daily Democrat*, Aug. 6, 1901.

Perry, J.W., "The Name of Heck Thomas Once A Terror To Outlaws," Lawton (Okla.) *Constitution*, Aug. 22, 1912.

Richardson, Grant, "The New Express Messenger," __, *Sunday Post Dispatch Magazine*, __, 1900.

"Riot Occurs In Game Tent," Lawton (O.T.) *Daily Democrat*, Aug. 6, 1901.

"SHOT HAWKINS," Lawton, 1904.

Steven, William P., "Walter Ferguson's Last 'News Tip' Brings Story of Early Outlaw Days," Tulsa *Tribune*, Mar. 15, 1936.

Thomas, Mrs. Heck, "The Law West of Fort Smith," *The Oklahoma News*, Feb. 12, 1939.

"True Tales of Men Whose Lives Overflow With Danger," *The Daily Oklahoman*, Jan. 7, 1911.

Upchurch, C. Winn, "Heck Thomas, Gentleman Lawman," *Oklahoma's Orbit*, Apr. 15, 1973.

Upchurch, C. Winn, "The Real Heck Ramsey," Atlanta (Ga.) *Constitution and Journal*, Feb. 18, 1873.

"Veteran Confederates Will Attend Inaugural Ceremonies," Nov. 15, 1907.

"Veteran Officer Given Summons," Lawton *Daily News and Star*, Aug. 16, 1912.

"Whole Family Helped Pioneer Preacher," Tulsa *Sunday World*, May 24, 1959.

2. Undated Clippings, Thomas Papers

"Battle of Atlanta," Atlanta *Constitution*.
"But Few Changes After all," Lawton.
"Dinner for Their Friends," Lawton.

"Of the Death of General Kerney," Atlanta.
"Doolin's Body In State," Guthrie.
"Father of City Sheriff Thomas, Shown In Picture At Theatre," Atlanta.
"Fireman's Ball A Success," Lawton (O.T.).
"General Edward Lloyd Thomas," Atlanta.
Gore, Ira, "Atlanta Man the Hero of Many Border Fights," Atlanta.
"Heck Thomas."
"Heck Thomas Goes To Grave Scarred In Many Combats."
"Heck Thomas Goes To Home In Lawton," Oklahoma City.
"Heck Thomas Is Very Ill," Lawton.
"Heck Thomas Requests Old Friends to "Send No Flowers," Guthrie.
"Heck Thomas' Reward," Guthrie.
"Heck Thomas Very Low," Lawton.
"Heroes of Oklahoma."
"Hunting the Daltons."
"A Fire Narrowly Averted Saturday," Lawton.
"An Atlanta Man Going to Klondike," Atlanta.
"Indian Fighter Here."
"Judge Parker's Marshals."
Langston, Carol, "Wind Moans Past Grave of 'King of Oklahoma Outlaws.'"
"Many Incidents and Faces are Recalled As Pioneers Meet Here," Tulsa.
"Many View the Body of Once Chief of Police," Lawton.
"Marshal Thomas Receives A Beautiful Medal From A Concourse of Friends," Lawton.
"Must Be Real Detectives," Guthrie.
"Part the Forty-Second Georgia Played," Atlanta.
"Perry Sixty Days Old."
"Police Record," Lawton.
Randolph, William N., "Heck Thomas, Oklahoma Officer, Unafraid."
"Resident of Lawton and Ex-Chief of Police Succumbed This Morning," Lawton.
"Revenue of Police Court," Lawton.
"Sham Bank Robbery, Famous Actors Play Leading Parts."
"Thomas Goes Home to Lawton."
"Thomas Receives a Role," Guthrie.
"Thomas' Reward."
"Thomas Thanks Friends," Lawton.
"Throngs Follow Thomas Body to City Cemetery," Lawton.

"To the Editor," Atlanta , (death of General Kearney).
"Will Commemorate Battle of Atlanta," Atlanta.

J. MICROFILM: OKLAHOMA STATE HISTORICAL SOCIETY

"Appointment," *The Edmond Sun-Democrat*, Nov. 12, 1897, 2/1.
"Biography on Death, Heck Thomas," *The Daily Oklahoman*, Aug. 18, 1912, 11/3-4.
"Biography, Edward Lloyd Thomas," Guthrie *Daily Leader*, July 29, 1894, 3/1-3.
"Doolin, Dalton, Tilghman," *Cherokee Advocate* (I.T.), Apr. 25, 1894, 2/4.
"Doolin Reward," *The Daily Oklahoman*, Aug. 29, 1896, p. 4/4.
"Dynamite Dick," *El Reno News*, Nov. 6, 1896, p. 4/4.
"Escape - David Givens," *Indian Chieftain*, October 10, 1889, p. 3/2.
"Game Warden Cleveland County," *Lexington Leader*, June 25, 1909, p. 3/2.
"Heck Thomas, Birth of Son," *The Daily Leader*, Guthrie, Aug. 23, 1894, 4/4.
"Heck Thomas Uses Gun In Quarrel With Councilman Gregg of Perry," *The Daily Leader*, Guthrie, Feb. 25, 1894, 3/4.
"Jim Starr," *Indian Chieftain*, Vinita, Jan. 30, 1890, 3/4.
"Line of Duty," *Indian Chieftain*, Vinita, Jan. 9, 1890, 3/2.
"Oscar Colin," *Indian Chieftain*, Vinita, Aug. 29, 1889, 3/3.
"Tilghman, Appointment," Stillwater *Gazette*, Nov. 11, 1897, p. 2/2.
"Timber Poachers," *Daily Oklahoma State Capitol*, July 19, 1893, ½.
"Story, Heck Thomas," *The Daily Oklahoman*, Nov. 10, 1935.

INDEX

5th Georgia Infantry, 10
35th Georgia Volunteers, 10
42nd Georgia Regiment, 14

A.P. Hill Camp V.C.V., 97, 138
Abernathy, John, 106-109 128-129, 132, 134
Archer, Annie, 109, 141
Archer, James, 141
Archer, Thomas Jefferson "Jeff," 47, 109-110
Askew, State Game Warden, 132

Baby Heck, 76, 78
Bass gang, 24
Bass, Sam, 3, 23-24, 134
Battle of Peachtree Creek, 15
Battle of Chantilly, 1, 12
Bedell, Edward, 7
Bedell, Martha Ann Fullwood, 7
Bedell, Pendleton, 7, 9-10
Bedell, Robert, 7
Billingslea, Frank, 146
Bland, Owen, 51
Blanding, H.R., 88, 99
Boles, Thomas, 38
Bruce, Bill, 88
Bushyhead, Dennis, 53

Carroll, John, 39, 43
Casey gang, 136
Caudel, Joe, 58

Christie, Ned, 136
Cleveland, Grover, 38, 65
Clinton, Charley, 17
Cobb's Legion, 10
Collins, Joel, 24
Cornish, W. K., 25
Couch, William, 59
Courtright, Jim, 31
Cox, Burrell, 64
Crane, Benjamin E., 22
Crawford, George W., 9
Cross Timbers, 24, 26
Cruce, Lee, 139
Curtis, W.E., 128

D.R. Volunter Company, 95
Dale, Judge Frank, 66
Dalton, Bob, 63-64, 66
Dalton, Emmett, 63-64, 139
Dalton, Frank, 63
Dalton gang, 3, 136
Dalton, Grat, 63-64, 134
Davis, President Jeff, 9
Dean, Marie A., 104-105
Diffendaffer, J.M., 143
Dodge, Fred, 64
Doolin, Bill, 3, 63, 66-67, 69-76 134, 136, 144-145
Drake, Lauren, 68
Duke of Norfolk, 7
Dunlap, Dr., 140-141

Edward, Joe, 126
Egan, Sheriff "Dad," 24

Elrod, Sam, 88
Ewing, Judge Amos, 90

Fighting Quartermaster, 10
Fort Worth Detective Association, 31
Forty-ninth Georgia, 1
Fossett, William D., 81-84, 76
Foster, Harry, 88
Foster, Perry, 87, 99
Fox and Sac Agency, 3, 5
Fullwood, Belle, 118

Gate City to the South, 14
Gentry, William, 89
Georgia 35th Infantry, 2
Geronimo, Chief, 97
Gibson, Ed, 131
Goff, Al, 89
Goff, Alva, G., 136
Gone With the Wind, 15
Goo Goo Avenue, 82-83
Gore, Thomas, 88, 90-981, 134
Gould, Jay, 23
Graham, Mrs. D.C., 141
Grant, President, 35
Gray, Isabelle "Belle," 18
Gray, Jennie, 9
Gray, Rev. Albert, 18-19, 43
Gregg, Councilman, 67
Grimes, Marshal, 136

Haden, D.A., 136
Hamond, Leka, 88
Hamonds, Charles, 88
Hanging Judge Parker, 35
Harley Thomas, 3
Harper's Ferry, 1-2, 13
Harrison, Benjamin, 53

Hawkins, Colonel Will, 99, 102-105
Hawkins, J.W. "Bill," 88- 89
Heatherington, 88
Hemphill, Robert, A.
Holliday, Sir Thomas, 7
Hood, General, 16
Houston & Texas Central Railway Co., 30
Ireland, Gov. John, 33
Irwin, Rev. R.T., 143
Isbell, L.P., 55-57
Iturbide, 9

Jacobs, Clerk, 99
Jacobson, A., 136
Jennings, Al, 76, 90, 110,128-129
Jennings gang, 76
Jennings, John, 90
Jennings, Lizzie, 90
Johnston, General, 16
Jones, Dick, 119
Jones, Mayor, 29, 121, 126
Jones, Press, 99-100, 109
Joy, C.G., 143

Kearney, Gen. Phillip, 2, 12-13
Kilpatrick, General, 14

La Fors, Rufus, 88
Lancaster, S. B., 88
Lantznester, John, 126, 138, 142-143
Larrance, Fred, 88
Lawton Confederate Veterans, 96
Ledbetter, Bud, 76
Lee, Gen. Robert E., 2, 10, 12-

13
Lee, Jim, 31-33
Lee, Pink, 31-33
Lee, Samuel, 14
Lord Mayor of London, 7
Lord Mowbray of England, 47
Loux, Charley, 99

Madsen, Chris, 3, 4, 61-62, 65-66, 87, 114-117, 129-130, 134, 136-137, 141, 143, 145
Madsen, Reno, 4, 114
Maledon, George, 35
Maples, Dan, 53, 55
Markeson, Mike, 138
Mary Queen of Scots, 7
Masterson, Bat, 61
McClamant, Robert, 131
McEachin, John, 58
McKinley, President, 79, 85, 90
McNolly, James, 58
Meeks, Beth Thomas, ix-x, 2, 3, 5, 132-133, 137-138, 142, 144 146
Mitchel, Margaret, 15
Morton, D.R., 88
Mowbray, Annie, 47
Mowbray, George, 110
Mowbray, George, Jr., 47
Mowbray, Mrs. Hannah, 47, 110, 141
Mowbray, Lord, 110
Mowbray, Matie, ix-x, 47-52, 111-113, 127-128, 132-133, 141-144
Mowbray, Rev. George, 47-48, 51, 110, 132, 138
Murphy, W.M., 98

Ned Christie, 53-58
Newlin, H.P., 46,48
Nix, Evett Dumas, 65

Oglesby, June G., 19
Oklahoma Boomers, 59
Oklahoma Highway Patrol, 145
Oklahoma Mutoscope Company, 128
Olds, Fred, 145
Ox Hill, 12

Pacific Express Company, 23
Painter, W. W., 85
Parker, Chief Quannah, 129
Parker, Isaac C., 35-36
Parker, Judge Isaac C., 2, 49
Payne, David, 59
Peak, Junis "June," 29
Pender's Division, 10
Pierce Institute, 44
Pink Lee gang, 3, 134
Pocohantas, 7
Porter, Joe, 15
Powell, Reverend, 44
Prince of Hangmen, 35
Purdy, Aaron, 45-46, 49
Purdy gang, 45
Purdy, Tom, 45

Quinette, W.H., 79

Radley, L.M., 119, 124
Rhinehart, Frank, 76
Roff, Alva, 31
Rolfe, James, 7
Roosevelt, 85, 106, 109, 12, 129-130
Ross, Lesly, P., 87

Rusk, Deputy, 55
Russell, T.A., 102-105

Salmon, Deputy, 55
Sattles, Jim, 33
Scissortail, 136
Scissortail, 4
Scott, Randolph, 146
Second Battle of Manassas, 11-12
Shaffer, Miss, 82
Sheppard, Sim, 124, 143
Sherman, General 14, 16
Signor, Henry, 89
Simmons, Britt, 58
Simmons, Sam, 58
Smith, Jack, 17
Sneed, R. A., 143
Spotsswood, Tom, 25
St. Anthony's Hospital, 123, 140
Stevens, Robert, 143
Stovall Brigade, 11
Stovepipe Hill, 48

Taylor, Jim, 32, 34
Texas Express Company, 2, 21, 23-24, 30-31
"The Bank Robbery," 129
The Big Pasture, 106, 128
The Big Fire, 100-101
The Flying Lady, 82
The Three Guardsmen, 3, 61-62, 65, 129
Thomas, Albert, 68, 77-78, 118, 120, 123, 135
Thomas, Belle Fullwood, 43-45, 69
Thomas, Beth, 3, 78, 87, 110-115, 118, 123-124, 127
Thomas, Charley, 10
Thomas, Col. Bud, 10, 14-16
Thomas, Edward Lloyd, Jr. 8
Thomas, Edward, 10
Thomas, Gen. Edward Lloyd, 2, 69, 77
Thomas, Harley, 3, 77, 87, 110-115, 118, 127, 132-133, 138, 144
Thomas, Heck , ix, 2-6, 11-13 (Second Battle of Manassas), 17 (receivd nickname), 18, (Brush Arbor Riot), 19-20, 21-23 (Texas frontier), 25-29, 31 (Fort Worth DetectiveAssociation), 32-33 (Pink Lee gang) (Sam Bass gang), 39-46 (Deputy, Parker's court), 44-46 (Purdy gang), 47-52 (romance), 55-58 (Ned Christie), 59-61 (Oklahoma Territory), 63-65 (Al Jennings gang), (Dalton gang), 67-69 (Perry), 95-97 (fire chief), 111-113 (chicken fighting), 115-116 (Battle of Peachtree Creek), 123+ (illness) 131-132 (defeated), 137-142 (final illness and death), 143-144 (funeral)
Thomas, Henry, 10
Thomas, Henry Gray, 19
Thomas, Henry (son), 118, 123, 125, 135
Thomas, Henry Phillip, 8, 10
Thomas, Henry, Lovick, 68
Thomas, Henry "Heck," 1,7

Thomas, Hon. Francis, 7
Thomas, James L. "Jim," 21-22, 24-26
Thomas, Lovick Pierce, 7- 11, 14
Thomas, Lovick Pierce, Jr., 9, 10
Thomas, Lovick Howard, 44
Thomas, Matie, 3, 6, 68, 77, 87, 91- 92, 99, 107-108,
Thomas, Nathaniel, 7
Thomas, Pamelia, 43
Thomas, Phillip, 7
Thomas, Rev., 9
Thomas, Rev. Edward Lloyd, 8
Thomas, Scott, 10
Thomas, Thomas, 7
Thomas, Wesley Wailes, 8, 10
Thompson and Waite General Merchandise, 43
Thompson, Canada H., 92
Thompson, Marshal, 79
Tilghman, Bill, 3, 39, 61-62, 65-67 76, 87, 111, 117,123, 129-130, 143, 145
Trainor, Bub, 55, 58
Tuttle, Hon. J.K., 99

Unassigned Lands, 59-60

Verdigris Kid, 136
Victor, S. G., 139

Walker, Gen.,15
Walker, T.S., 125
Wells Fargo Express Co., 23, 64
West, Little Dick, 76
Whirlwind, Chief, 114-117

Whitaker, Andy, 17
Whitaker, Jared I., 17
White Bead Hill, 43-44
William the Conqueror, 47
Woody, A.S., 88
Wright, Frank, 90, 99
Wylie, A.C. and B.F., 19, 21

Yoes, Jacob, 53, 55, 57-59